D. Morris Kurtz

Ithaca and its Resources

Being an Historical and Descriptive Sketch of the....

D. Morris Kurtz

Ithaca and its Resources
 Being an Historical and Descriptive Sketch of the....

ISBN/EAN: 9783337096090

Printed in Europe, USA, Canada, Australia, Japan

Cover: Foto ©ninafisch / pixelio.de

More available books at **www.hansebooks.com**

BEING AN HISTORICAL AND DESCRIPTIVE SKETCH OF THE "FOREST CITY"
AND ITS MAGNIFICENT SCENERY.

GLENS, FALLS, RAVINES,

CORNELL UNIVERSITY,

AND THE PRINCIPAL

MANUFACTURING AND COMMERCIAL INTERESTS.

BY

D. MORRIS KURTZ.

FULLY ILLUSTRATED.

Ithaca, N. Y.:
Journal Association Book and Job Print.
1883.

Copyright by
D. Morris Kurtz
1883.

PREFACE.

When work was begun on ITHACA AND ITS RESOURCES it was my intention to devote a large share of my space to the history of Ithaca, but upon consultation with several prominent citizens, it was deemed advisable that, as the history of Ithaca had been written several times, more or less accurately, and as those features which should give to Ithaca a national, a world-wide reputation, have been neglected, less space should be devoted to the history and more to a description of its magnificent scenery—its attractive surroundings. Accordingly I have given largely of my space to a description of Ithaca and its surroundings—fully aware of the fact, however, that my feeble attempt in this direction cannot do it justice and may not prove satisfactory to readers or critics—merely outlining the history of the village and dividing the entire space as nearly equal as possible between the description of its surroundings and its resources. Cornell University forming a subject of deep interest to every resident of Ithaca, as well as to many people throughout the State and land, claimed largely my attention, but I do not think any one will regret that so much space has been given the noble institution. Of the sketches relating to its resources—the manufacturing and mercantile interests of Ithaca—little else need be said than that the statements made therein can be relied upon as being only just and accurate. Many, in fact nearly all, of the sketches relating to the mercantile interests were written by a gentleman residing in Ithaca and possessing an intimate acquaintance with its merchants, and his instructions were "be careful that no statements are made that you cannot substantiate," and I believe they were fully carried out. Of course it was impossible within the limits of the work to review *every* manufacturing and mercantile establishment, but an opportunity was given *every leading* manufacturer and merchant to be represented in the book, and I regret that a few did not avail themselves of the opportunity; but I am pleased to state that the number of those thus refusing to do their part towards making the work complete and a success are very few indeed, and I feel that it is complete without them—that the showing made by the enterprising representatives of the industrial and commercial interests, who availed themselves of the opportunity, reflects the greatest credit upon themselves and the "Forest City," and that no exceptions can be taken to my assertions. Although written very hurriedly, I have been careful to verify such statements as might be questioned, and am confident that the entire work is as reliable and accurate as such a book can be made. Where so many have given their encouragment and assistance, it is impossible to make personal mention of each, and, therefore, I will conclude these prefatory remarks by simply saying that all who have aided me by either word or deed have my sincerest thanks.

D. M. K.

ITHACA, October, 1883.

	PAGE		PAGE
Location and Surroundings,	7–11	Wortman & Son,	87–88
Ithaca Gorge,	11–16	C. H. VanHouter,	88
Glenwood,	16–19	J. F. Bruen,	88–89
Taghanic,	19–22	R. A. Heggie,	89
Buttermilk Creek,	22–24	White & Burdick,	89–90
Enfield Falls,	24–26	The Patrick Wall Shoe Store,	90
Lick Brook,	26–27	The Autophone Company,	90–93
Six Mile Creek and Other Falls,	27–28	C. A. Ives,	93
Cascadilla Glen,	28–29	Sheldon & Bliven,	93–94
Cornell University,	30–52	C. S. Wixom	94
Early History of Ithaca,	52–57	William Frear,	94–95
Its Churches,	57	Reynolds & Lang,	95–96
Public Schools,	57–58	J. H. Horton,	96
Its Newspapers,	58–61	Andrus & Church,	97–98
Public Buildings and Grounds,	61–62	Ithaca Glass Works,	98–100
Local Government,	62	E. S. Esty & Sons,	100–102
Water and Gas,	62	The Ithaca Sign Works,	102
Its Facilities and Resources,	62–63	Ithaca Telephone Service,	102–103
The Forest City Mixed Paint Works,	63–65	William M. Culver,	103–104
		Shepherd & Doyle,	104
The Ithaca Calendar Clock Co.,	65–69	Post, Sharp & Co.,	104–108
Marsh & Hall,	69–70	Geo. Griffin,	108
C. J. Rumsey & Co.,	70–71	Enz & Miller,	108–109
J. C. Stowell & Son,	71–72	Ackley's News Room,	109
Henry Bool,	72–75	The Boston Variety Store,	109
Hawkins, Todd & Co.,	75–76	Mrs. L. A. Burritt,	109–110
Ithaca Manufacturing Works,	76–78	A Record of Fifty Years,	
Uri Clark,	78–79	G. W. Hoysradt,	110–111
Ithaca Gun Works,	79–80	Finch & Apgar,	111
The West End Drug Store,	80–81	Andrews & Aldrich,	111–112
Jackson & Bush,	81–82	George Rankin & Son,	112–113
The Clinton House,	82–84	John Northrup,	113–114
H. V. Bostwick,	84	E. W. Prager,	114–115
George Small,	84–85	Nourse & Dederer,	115
A. B. Wood,	85	Jamieson & McKinney,	115–116
Dr. F. S. Howe,	86	Central N. Y. Accident and Relief Association,	116
R. C. Christiance,	86–87		

CONTENTS.

	PAGE		PAGE
Harrison Howard,	116	Paris & Emig,	119
The Ithaca Hotel,	117	W. H. Willson,	120
Thomas F. Doherty,	118	J. T. Morrison,	120-121
Tompkins House,	118	James Quigg,	121
E. K. Johnson,	118	H. M. Straussman,	121-122
F. W. Brooks,	119	Conclusion,	122

ILLUSTRATIONS.

Mouth of Fall Creek	9	The New Chemical and Physical Laboratory	43
Ithaca Fall, Ithaca Gorge	11		
The mouth of the Tunnel	12	Sage Chapel	45
Forest Fall, Ithaca Gorge	13	Ezra Cornell	47
Glenwood	16	The President's House	50
Taghanic Falls	21	The Journal Block	59
Ravine in Buttermilk Creek	23	Ithaca Calendar Clock Works	66-67
Enfield Ravine	25	Bool's Buildings	74
Enfield Falls	27	The Clinton House	83
Third Fall, Lick Brook	29	Autophones	92
Cornell University Campus	31	Ithaca Glass Works	99
A View of the University at an Earlier Period	35	Post, Sharp & Co's. Road and Village Carts	106
The Sage College for Women	39	The Ithaca Hotel	117

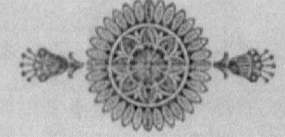

LYING between two hills, the summits of which tower about seven hundred feet above it on either side, Cayuga Lake, forty miles in length, from a mile and a half to five miles wide, and from one hundred to four hundred feet in depth, is like—to use an inelegant comparison—"an immense trough cut in the great plateau or backbone of Central New York." The hill on the west divides Cayuga from Seneca, and the water it sheds is distributed into the two lakes; that on the east forms the water shed between Cayuga and the Tioughnioga River, and the hills closing it in at the southern extremity divide their waters between the lake and the Susquehanna River. At the head of Cayuga a tract of land nearly level, two miles long and one and a half wide, extends south from the lake shore, the hills surrounding it on the south, east and west rising rather abruptly to a height of several hundred feet. Upon this plain and the adjacent hillslopes is built the village of Ithaca.

The entire descent from the great table land to the lake level is from 700 to 900 feet, of which 400 to 600 feet are accomplished within the last mile of distance. The soil of this bottom land is a rich, deep alluvium, and was in ages past covered by the waters of the lake, shells having been found on the hillsides at a height of 40 and 50 feet which were undoubtedly left there by the receding waters. Through the village wind their way, forming the head waters of Cayuga lake, the streams which, having come rushing, tumbling, thundering down the hills, now so quietly meander along as though bereft of their power, exhausted by their rough and perilous journey toward the calm and peaceful lake: Fall, Cascadilla, Six Mile, Buttermilk and Enfield Creeks, the four latter mingling their limpid waters with the deep and sluggish Cayuga Inlet, which, after reaching the lowlands, is of sufficient depth for nearly a mile before emptying into the lake to float the steamers plying upon it.

The streams in their course from the table lands to the lake have worn deep channels in the rocks, and the waterfalls which were once, probably, at the face of the bluffs, have receded in some instances more than a mile, forming below deep, rocky chasms bordered by perpendicular walls. The rocks are composed of strata of different degrees of hardness, and the water has worn them irregularly, the soft and yielding shales generally forming a declining surface, while the hard and compact limestone retains its perpendicular form. Thus it happens that the hills surrounding Ithaca on the east, south and west, which from a distance charm the eye with scenes of quiet beauty, verdant slope and sunny woodland, contain within their bosoms in form of glen and rock and waterfall, a wealth of wonders which cannot elsewhere be found in so small a compass.

Within ten miles of Ithaca there are one hundred and fifty waterfalls—cascades and cataracts. Found in dark gorges and in beautiful glens, all of them accessible, each one possessing peculiar features of interest in connection with its surroundings, many with special characteristics which, independent of the rest, attract visitors and captivate them by the beauties and grandeur presented, nowhere east of the Rocky Mountains has nature been more lavish with her gifts of wonder and awe-inspiring scenery.

Ithaca itself, apart from these attractions, is worthy of note as being the most picturesque and beautiful village in the State of New York. Clustered here on this level plain and hills surrounding is a community of nearly 12,000 people. Down on the "flat" broad streets cross each other at right angles and are lined on either side by umbrageous trees, with overhanging branches and variegated leaves. Handsome residences, well-kept lawns and pretty little parks add much to its attractiveness, and the business portion of the village is marked by spacious brick blocks of imposing dimensions and architecture. The hills on the south, the east and the west are dotted with beautiful villas, elegant mansions and pretty cottages, while crowning the summit of the East Hill are the magnificent structures of Cornell University. The view from any of these points is picturesque in the extreme, but probably more comprehensive and charming from the hills on the south. Almost rivalling the far-famed "Switchback" at Mauch Chunk, in Pennsylvania, entering Ithaca from the south over the Delaware, Lackawanna and Western Railroad is one of the greatest pleasures yet reserved for the tourist, for strange as it may seem, with all its attractions of rock, glen, waterfall and lake scenery, this beautiful village is but little frequented, comparatively, by these seekers after pleasure and novelty—and mainly from a lack of knowledge as to its existence, it probably never having been properly brought to their notice.

Running in a northwesterly direction from Owego, this railroad, upon reaching the summit of South Hill, first forms a letter N on the brow of the hill, then running around the hillside continues its descent in a southwesterly direction until it reaches the lowlands about two miles south of Ithaca, where it makes a large curve and returning through the Valley of the Inlet enters the village. As the cars reach the brow of the hill the traveller catches a bird's-eye view of Ithaca and Cayuga Lake framed in by hills covered with a wealth of foliage, and while backing down to the second switch he has a fine side view of East Hill and Cornell

ITHACA AND ITS RESOURCES. 9

MOUTH OF FALL CREEK.

University, with which he is nearly on a level. Then as the train again moves forward and continues its journey around the hillside another and a different view is presented for his admiration. On the level plain, a half mile below, is seen Ithaca, almost concealed by the tops of the trees by which its every street is lined, and to its superabundance of which it is indebted for the title of the "Forest City". The hill and the intervening space between is dotted by handsome residences, with sloping lawns and pretty shrubbery. In the west is another hill presenting a similar appearance, while still another, but this time full and unobstructed view, is obtained of the University Buildings in the east and the magnificent grounds by which they are surrounded. To the north stretches the placid waters of Cayuga Lake, that with its framing of bright foliage-covered hills and the inlet at its head, might be likened unto a large and beautiful hand mirror. As the train speeds on around the hill and away to the South, this picture is left behind, only to recur in part again when the return is made towards the village. And when the wondering traveller alights at his hotel he is surprised to learn that the distance which he traversed about five miles to accomplish, might have been accomplished by a pleasant walk of half a mile from the first switch down the hill, and in less time, too, than was required by his car. But this circuitous route is a wonderful improvement as compared with the two inclined planes up which cars were drawn by horse power many years ago, and the novelty of the trip, with its panoramic scenes, well repays for the vexation experienced by the hurried traveller when, anxious to be at his journey's end, he beholds the place at his very feet and is then carried away off from it, only to be compelled to retrace his steps, as it were, before being permitted to alight,—but his impatience is lost in admiration.

A beautiful village of itself, surrounded on every side by such wonders of nature as might well command the attention even of the experienced tourist who has visited the recognised wonders of the world, is it not strange that Ithaca has not already formed the Mecca to which those pilgrims ruled by fashion's sway annually seek the way? Surely this can only be attributable to that capricious dame's ignorance of the beautiful kingdom o'er which she might reign supreme with such honor to herself and pleasure to her subjects, were she but so inclined? But probably it is better as it is, for what could compensate for the loss of the peace and quiet now enjoyed, but which under her rule would be destroyed? One of the greatest charms of this delightful region lies in that sense of freedom from the domination of "society" and the absence of all that can disturb the true lover of the grand, beautiful and picturesque in nature in the full enjoyment of his pleasures.

Of the principal points of interest in "Our Scenery" a well known writer has said: "Rome boasted of her seven hills, from whose throne of beauty she ruled the world. Ithaca makes her boast of seven streams, concerning which she challenges the world. Each of these has a character of beauty peculiar to itself, so that they must all be seen to comprehend the perfect whole. Enfield is distinguished by its giddy, winding walk along the sides of the profound precipices. The ravine of Lick Brook is as utterly wild as the day when Ithaca was a log cabin under the hill; on the contrary, the explorer of Six Mile Creek emerges at brief intervals into the sight of farm houses and cultivated fields. The interest of Taghanic mainly centers in its magnificent fall, 215 feet in height; whereas the Cascadilla, as its beautiful name imports, is remarkable for its numerous smaller, though not less picturesque cascades, not many of them rising to the dignity and sublimity of falls. Fall Creek is distinguished by its broad and unfailing stream, which at all seasons goes sounding through its almost impassable gorge and casts itself headlong over the nearest and noblest of all our cataracts, the Ithaca Fall. Contrasted with this, is the untastefully, though not inaptly named, Buttermilk Ravine, where the stream is so shallow and at the same time distributes itself so widely over the rocks as to partake of the foamy whiteness belonging to the product of the churn, rather than of the spring."

But let me be your guide and we will visit each in turn, sail upon the lake and enjoy a couple weeks of this golden October month in a Bohemian manner. And if, when your vacation is at an end, you do not partake of my enthusiasm and register a vow to return here year after year and refresh your body with quiet and rest amidst these scenes of glen and rock and waterfall, the memory of which should pleasantly haunt you; your mind with those better thoughts which this communion with nature—leading you irresistibly to "turn your eyes from nature up to nature's God"—forces upon you; then your "bump of veneration" is very flat, indeed, and I would rather you went not with me. As one of the most attractive features of this "ramble" will be the great variety of striking objects and characteristics presented in the different glens and ravines, they will be visited

ITHACA FALL, ITHACA GORGE—150 FEET.

in the order in which this diversity is best illustrated, and we will accordingly wend our way, first, to

ITHACA GORGE.

"The Gorge is the strange, hidden enjoyment of a leaf out of Switzerland, almost in the streets of the town," said a writer in the New York *World* some years ago, and when, after a short walk down Aurora street, we stand on the neat iron bridge spanning Fall Creek and gaze up into Ithaca Gorge, we feel that it is but a step from civilization into the depths of a wilderness. Alongside us the Fall Creek manufactories; in front a dark, deep ravine. Pausing a moment to listen to the roar of the waters and fix this picture in our minds—a foaming cataract, 150 feet in height and just as broad, with cliffs towering an hundred feet above it on either side, the water circling round a dark eddy at its base, thence struggling out a narrow stream through the great shadowy defile into the sunlight, and passing under our feet, murmuringly continuing its journey to the lake—we will enter the pretty little lodge guarding the entrance to the Gorge, and pass on up to a broad terrace, from which we obtain a more charming view—to the left this beautiful Ithaca Fall; to the right the village. Pouring over the jagged rocks in a snow white and flowing veil, the water in its descent resembles the bridal veil of some fair young maiden being led to the altar, and is indescribably beautiful. But were we so fortunate as to visit the fall just after a freshet, we would see a "scene which no equal section of Niagara could surpass, so vast the volume of water, so dark and sullen its hue; besides its peculiar efflorescent appearance as it broke against the ragged cliff in its descent, a lofty column of spray rose like the smoke of a conflagration at its foot and almost hid the entire front of the Fall—above all, a gorgeous rainbow spanned the stream, rising in a perfect arch higher than the Fall itself." Following the walk winding midway along the almost perpendicular hillside, up and down, we come upon another terrace, from which a finer full view is obtained. The Fall has continued to grow in impressiveness as we approach, and seems higher and wider and its noise more deafening. The mills and the village have passed out of sight, and shut in by trees on every side, except that which opens towards the Falls, here is a place to lie and dream the summer's day away. On the left is a vast ampitheatre formed by perpendicular rocks, which rise three or four hundred feet from the bed of the stream. At our feet lies the dark, deep water, made almost black by the shadows cast from the cedars covering the face of the rocky wall across. And as our eyes wander from the Fall to the giant palisade stretching northward from the cataract and towering far above all the rest, we are filled with awe at the majesty of the scene. Continuing our walk, the path leads us aound the ampitheatre, thickly shaded at all times, and through the trees we catch glimpses of the water as it bounds down the ragged wall. Then ascending a rocky staircase of about twenty steps, we reach a plateau on a level with the Falls; a few steps across the shady plot and we stand on the brink, gazing down at the water as it takes the awful leap into the basin a hundred and fifty feet below. If the water in the stream above were low, we might climb down into the rocky bed of the Falls, and while standing on the very edge and in the center of the cataract's highway, imagine how quickly would we be swept off and into eternity were the dam to burst its bonds and the imprisoned waters be loosed upon us. Or we might walk across the wall of the dam, a rod or two above the Falls, and passing through the Tunnel, step across the raging little stream on its way to turn the wheels of busy manufactories, and standing on Rock Island obtain still another and even grander view of the Falls, being almost directly over it, yet sufficiently in front to observe its whole surface.

The object of the tunnel was to bring the water of Fall Creek down to the mills and other factories located on the bluff and at its base. Many years ago, (when the first mills were erected here in 1814) a wooden flume, suspended on a frame work morticed in the rock, carried the water from a point above the Falls around the face of the bluff, and down to the mills. With the erection of other mills the supply of water thus furnished became inadequate for all, and in in 1830 J. S. Beebe, then one of the most enterprising citizens of the village and a large owner of mill property here, ordered the excavation of a tunnel.' "He had in his employ a poor, energetic but far seeing young man, now the Hon. Ezra Cornell [deceased, but alive in the memory of the people], who had entire charge of the work, and who in fact conceived it. At that time no blasting with gunpowder had ever been done at Ithaca, but young Cor-

FOREST FALL, ITHACA GORGE—60 FEET.

nell went down on the Cayuga and Seneca canal, where work of that kind was going on, and observed the process of rock blasting, hired an Irishman who was accustomed to rock drilling, and returned in two or three days, and with the aid of five men and 1,000 kegs of gunpowder, in about six months had this hole through the rocks, 15 feet high, 15 feet wide and 200 feet long." The rickety wooden flume was then abandoned, and the water has since been conducted from the dam then built above the Falls, through the tunnel and down a raceway cut in the solid rock to the veritable hive of industry below.

Having lingered longer than was intended around this "first fall", we will retrace our steps across the plateau and begin the ascent to the peak of the craggy rocks, more than a hundred feet aloft. The path winds around the amphitheatre, just above that by which we arrived at the plateau, for a short distance, and then by a zig-zag course conducts us to a point about fifty feet directly over the plateau, where we stop, draw a few long breaths and enjoy the impressive scene. And while you are looking down into the depths of the Gorge, watching the water take its fearful plunge, or tracing out the winding path by which we came, I will tell you a little story—one which has retained its original form despite the numerous tellings. See the path before us, hewn in the solid rock, and rising along the naked perpendicular cliff, only wide enough for a single pedestrian ? On the 24th of August, 1869, Mr. John Johnson, a resident of Ithaca, was at work alone on this path, and while prying on a crow bar, with his back to the chasm below, his hold slipped and he fell back and headlong down the precipice, the bar following him ! Down, down, he went, 200 feet, the iron bar ringing out as it struck the rocks and followed after him ! But once he struck, and then some loose dirt about fifty feet below us; then one long jump of a hundred and fifty feet and he fell on the soft ground near the basin at the foot of the Fall. Will you believe it, he picked up the crow bar, looked around for his hat and was soon again at his work! Now let us follow that path, and ascending a long stairway cut in the solid rocks we stand on the brink of a precipice more than three hundred feet higher than the point from which we started—the bridge on which we stood and saw such a pretty picture. Beneath us a frightful chasm ; before us the valley, with the silvery streams winding their way to the Lake. Ah! step not too close, lest your head swirl, down you go nearly 200 feet, and I will have another story to tell. A few feet further on another crag juts out twenty or thirty feet from the mainland, and standing on its head we have another picture similar to the one we first looked at, only the cataract is not so high nor wide as the Ithaca Fall, nor the cliffs rising on either side so tall. Forest Fall is only 60 feet high, but the volume of water is greater and the ravine beyond looks darker and more gloomy. Great fissures in this crag suggest thoughts of its early disruption, and as we wander along the precipice we are filled with wonder. How long, think you, has been required to wear out this great path through the rocks by this once insignificent stream? Through a thicket of pines our path thence leads, and we descend into the bowels of the Gorge by a winding way, rather steep and rocky, but made comparatively easy by the enthusiasm our "ramble" thus far has created. As we emerge from a second amphitheatre and stand on the verge of this second fall, we are thrilled with the wild beauty of the scene—shut in on one side by the cliffs, rising to a great height and covered with moss and ferns and shrubbery clinging tenaciously to their sides ; on the other by a great high hill, its precipitous bank bedecked with the brightest colored foliage, the water pours over the fall with an awful roar and then quietly flows on through the Gorge and disappears from our view—looking in the other direction only the bright stream, laughing and dancing on its way, as though happy in its sombre surroundings, is to be seen through the trees. But we follow the path along the bed of the stream only a little way when the voice of another fall gives greeting, and a brighter scene is presented. This is Foaming Fall, 30 feet high. Here the Gorge seems wider and the sun shining down on the water, lights up a picture made brilliant with color by the variegated leaves on the trees. Descending into the bed of the stream we walk close up to the fall and receive a shower of spray from the foaming little cataract. It is shaped like a $\wedge$, the water shooting from each side down into the centre and being lashed into foam by the contention, but little escaping to flow over the lower ends of the fall directly into the stream below, and is very curious. Climbing to the path and again following its tortuous windings, along the bank, we soon hear the thunder of the fourth fall, and in a few minutes stand on the verge of Rocky Fall, 55 feet in height. This fall crosses the stream at an angle and is very wide. The action of the water when at its flood has worn a great hollow into the soft rock wall on the south side, which serves as an immense sounding board, and the roar of the water is thus more than doubled in volume. At the foot of the fall on the north side has been placed a turbine wheel, and the power furnished by the rushing water is transmitted by an endless wire cable to the Mechanical Department of Cornell University, on the hill 200 feet above. Although it has not, apparently, the same charm as the others, we linger some time at Forest Fall before resuming our walk, probably because we are rather tired, and as we sit and muse and become accustomed to the roar, it fascinates us, our limbs refuse to move, and it is only by an effort that we throw off the abstraction and turn away from the spot. But then we are refreshed, and when we enter the beautiful glen through which the path leads, we can all the more fully enjoy its scenes of quiet woodland beauty. The ravine has widened out, and on either side the rippling waters, for the first time since the Gorge was entered, we find a narrow but level stretch of land. The cliffs have disappeared, and instead, steep hills covered with a dense growth of trees and shrubbery, tower two or three hundred feet above us. Moss and ferns and evergreens are all around our path, and here we could wander about for hours with constantly increasing delight, but there are yet other and even more attractive scenes awaiting, and we must hasten onward. As we near the end of this "Sylvan Glen", the Gorge again begins to narrow, and were the water not so low we would be compelled to follow the path up and around the high ledge of rocks jutting out in front of us, but as it is we take to the bed of the stream and rounding this point enter the "Colosseum," one of the most interesting features of the Gorge. It is a perfect ampitheatre of immense proportions—hundreds of feet in diameter. The circular walls are formed by the perpendicular cliffs rising to a height of between one and two hundred feet and worn out thus round by the action of the whirling waters in ages past. Through a small opening in the rocky wall at the further end the entire volume of Fall Creek pours down forty feet into the basin, and then finds its way out through the narrow pass by which we entered, and the only natural entrance to this wonder of nature's wonders. In its fall a portion of the water strikes a mass of rock jutting out near the base, scattering it in a huge boquet of foam flowers and forming the prettiest fall in the Gorge. The reverberation of the falling water's roar is almost deafening, and from its regular and answering beat has arisen the name of Triphammer Falls. The rocky bottom of the Colosseum is level as a floor ; above can only be seen a fringe of trees peeping over the edge of the precipice and the clear, calm, blue sky. A few years ago we would have been compelled to turn back, retrace our steps through the Gorge, before finding an exit, but we can now ascend a spiral staircase and soon stand alongside the flume cut by nature in the solid rock, and which conducts the water through these narrows to Triphammer Falls and into the "Colosseum". Here the student of nature will find much to interest him—moldings carved by the water that are beyond the skill of man to surpass; great holes in the rocks, perfect in symmetry and resembling huge punch-bowls and cauldrons, and other curiosities of like nature. With an admiring glance at the beautiful Flume Fall above, 26 feet in height, we climb out of the "flume" and crossing the frail foot bridge spanning the chasm directly over Triphammer Fall, start on our return to the village. It would be a pleasure to explore the romantic-looking ravine above the sixth fall, but the day is far spent and this must be reserved until we have visited Glenwood, Taghanic, Enfield and other points of interest, when you can at your leisure—as you certainly will desire—more fully inspect those spots that especially attract your attention. From Triphammer and Flume Falls our path leads along the top of the precipice forming the south side of the Gorge for half or three quarters of a mile ; through the trees and shrubbery we catch frequent glimpses of the bright stream below; **the roar of** Triphammer accompanies us, and **has not** yet become indistinct before that of Forest Fall breaks upon our ears; and thus we have a continual reminder of the wild scenes through which we have come until we reach the beautiful grounds of **Cornell University.** With but passing **glances** at the noble structures adorning the elegant campus, for we shall pay this spot a lengthy visit previous to our departure from **Ithaca,** we follow the walk south to the Cascadilla bridge, stopping a moment, however, to observe the "Sunset on the Lake". A picture of surpassing beauty? **Ah,** yes! Down in the valley lies the "Forest City", almost hid by the gold and cardinal-tinted leaves on the tall trees lining its streets; just north Cayuga Lake, the hills surrounding brilliant with the same highly-colored foliage; gradually disappearing **behind these hills,** the sun sheds a soft, mellow light and reflects all the hues of the rainbow on the mirror-like surface of the Lake. At Cascadilla bridge again **we** stop and peering down into the cavernous gloom of the ravine, with a shudder turn away and continue around Cascadilla Place to West Buffalo street and down the hill, soon arriving again at Aurora street, whence we disperse to our hotels. Tired? Well yes, but after a refreshing sleep you will be ready in the morning for a sail upon the Lake, and

GLENWOOD.

At 9 o'clock in the morning, then, we step on board a comfortable little steam yacht lying at her dock foot of West Buffalo street, the lines are cast off and in a few minutes we are sailing up the Inlet. It is a bright, beautiful morning and our exercise of the **day previous gives us a feeling** of exhilaration which is a presage of the liveliest enjoyment. Rapidly leaving behind us the "Forest City", soon the long pier at the head of Cayuga is reached, and passing the lighthouse **we are out upon the bosom of the Lake.** Our little boat takes a northwesterly course and **as we near the** western shore we observe a pretty cottage built upon **the** sloping hillside. "What a **delightful** location for a summer residence," **is your** natural exclamation. **Then as we** steam northward **one after another of** these cottages are brought into view, **some** large and **roomy, others so small that** they seem like toys; some built upon a grassy **knoll, others down in a** little vale—but all of them possessing a charm that would **make our** occupancy **of** any of them during the summer months most enjoyable. At the foot of the slope fronting each is a tasty little boat-house; some of the cottagers row from their cottage to the village, some sail and others run their own steam yachts—but all add life and activity to the Lake on summer evenings. Extending out into the Lake just north of us is a long "point", the fine growth of trees on which is suggestive of picnics and excursion parties under their leafy branches. A short run **and** the little steamer **lays** alongside a dock built at the extreme **end of the "point",** is made fast and we land and look about us.

This is Glenwood, **four miles pleasant sailing, or five** miles driving over the hills, from Ithaca. The "point" is about **200** feet broad and extends 200 or 300 feet from the mainland **out into the Lake,** forming quiet little bays on each side of it. At the foot **of the hills is a** rustic hotel and passing around to the rear, we enter the beautiful glen from whence arises the name—Glenwood. Neither too long nor too broad, this glen is the ideal glen of our imagination. On either **side** the

GLENWOOD

hills slope from the level of the Lake to a height of about 150 feet. The sides of the glen, however, are rather precipitous, but with the bottom as well as the hill tops, are decked out in all the splendor of their autumn foliage. On its way to join the waters of the lake a babbling brook runs through the glen and we have followed it up not more than 300 feet, when our progress is barred by a high precipice. Through a narrow opening in its face, 50 feet below the top, the water pours in a glassy sheet, with a direct fall of about 20 feet, thence bounding down from rock to rock, accomplishes the remaining distance of 70 feet by a series of pretty cascades. A more charming woodland scene cannot be imagined. Returning through the glen to the hotel, we ascend the hill on the north, and arriving at the brink of this precipice again follow the course of the stream. Here it flows over a rocky bed through a miniature "Gorge", and a few steps brings us to the foot of the second fall. The characteristics of this fall are similar to that of the first, but it is not so high, the water falling only about 70 feet. From the second fall on up to the summit of the hill a succession of rapids and wooded dell make attractive our ramble, and when we return our dinner awaits us. The afternoon we will spend in rambling around the hills and sailing or rowing upon the lake, not neglecting to visit the Eastern shore just opposite. While engaged in this pleasurable pastime I will tell you of the contemplated improvements that will make this spot the most attractive summer resort on Cayuga Lake.

For years Glenwood has been the favorite haunt of "picnickers", and the evidences of their frequent visits are found in the numerous long tables occupying a large part of the shady "point". To picnic parties, it is probably unnecessary to state, an hotel is a secondary consideration, consequently the hotel here has not received the proper attention. But the 24 acres of land comprising Glenwood have recently been purchased by Mr. J. E. Van Natta, of Ithaca, who purposes transforming it from simply a picnic ground into the delightful place for spending the summer months for which the location and surroundings possess all the requisites. The old hotel will be removed and on its site erected a handsome and commodious new edifice. From beneath the trees on the "point" the picnic tables will be transferred to a desirable part of the glen, the attention of an efficient gardener given to creating in their stead an attractive lawn, and water conducted in pipes from the upper fall will play through pretty fountains scattered about these new grounds. On the bluffs north and south of the glen will be built several neat cottages, the roadway down the hill will be improved and more suitable accommodations provided for the horses and carriages of guests. Extending from the top of the hotel to the bluff on the north a unique but substantial dancing pavilion will be constructed, and—"last but not least," an experienced hotel man will be placed in charge of the "hostelrie", which, first-class in all its appointments will be conducted in first-class style, and "particular attention given to the *cuisine*." Here in this spot seemingly designed by nature expressly for this purpose, with such society as the high character of the establishment will naturally attract ; the days passed in boating, or fishing, or reading a favorite book in some quiet nook, with only the babbling brook or its noisy little waterfalls for company ; your night's slumber undisturbed by that nasty little pest, the mosquito ; do you not think in the hottest summer month it would be a perfect Elysium?

Again we are on board the little steamer, her prow pointed south-by-east and ploughing at a fine rate of speed through the water. Again the sun going down behind the hills lends charming effect to a brilliant picture, than which the brush of mortal artist could not more pleasingly depict. And when again we enter the sluggish waters of the Inlet, and the wild and the picturesque is lost in the commonplace of commerce and manufacture, we heave a sigh at the transition and look forward with pleasure to the morrow and its pilgrimage to the highest and most celebrated falls in this region—

TAGHANIC.

We have a choice of several very pleasant routes to Taghanic—by the lake steamers running between Ithaca and Cayuga, the Geneva, Ithaca and Sayre Railroad, or a carriage drive through an exceptionally fine agricultural region. We also have a choice of several ways of spelling and pronouncing the name—Taug-han nock, Taug-hanick, Tagh-kanic, Tag-hanic. As to the name, I choose the latter; route, the carriage drive over the hills. Behind a spanking team of horses—and good livery teams are to be obtained here—we drive down State street, across the Inlet and take the upper right hand road leading over the hill. The view of Ithaca and its surroundings, at which we tire not looking, is superb as we ascend the hill, and then one after another are passed the farms of evidently well-to-do tillers of the soil—fine cattle, large barns, handsome residences with well-kept lawns, neatly painted fences enclosing the rich looking land, all evince the greatest thrift and prosperity. The eight miles between Ithaca and Jacksonville are only too quickly accomplished, then turning to the right, at the latter place, a short drive of two miles towards the lake brings us to a plain two-story frame building standing in the midst of a grove of pines, on the north side of the road. A signboard at the cross-road above had informed us that this was the way to the Cataract House at Taghanic Falls, but were it not for the conspicuous sign here displayed we would have remained unaware of our proximity to the falls and probably driven by with only an admiring glance at what we considered an attractive rural hotel with remarkably pretty grounds. That sign has set us right, however, and wheeling into the grove and alongside the piazza extending round the front of the house, we are courteously received by the proprietor, Mr. R. Mockford, relieved of the care of our horses and are ready for a sight at Taghanic. But where is it? We do not hear the thunder and roar that is inseparably associated with our ideas of great waterfalls. Rustic seats and arbors are plentifully scattered about the grove. Through a vista in front we see a large open space that is intuitively felt to be a great, deep gorge. Approaching, we stand on the brink of a precipice and gaze wonderingly down into this space, 600 feet wide and 400 feet in depth. Following the course of the stream running through the bottom with our eyes, they rest upon Cayuga the Fair, into which the Taghanic is emptying its mite. A pretty sight, indeed, the beautiful lake, whose calm and unruffled waters have been so stirred with strife before reaching this haven of rest. Are you equal to the task of descending into the gorge? It will repay you for the exertion. Then follow me along this dizzy zigzag path, which makes one-third of the descent comparatively easy.

At the end of the path an almost perpendicular stairway "assists" us down another hundred feet, and thence by many successive leaps we reach the bottom—for it is easier to leap than it is to carefully, step by step descend. Look up! How small and stunted appear the trees which, when we were on a level with their topmost branches but a few moments ago, looked to us like the tallest giants of the forest. Out into the middle of the gorge and look up. Can you realize that it is 400 feet to the top, where you see the bare spot among the trees whence we started? An "Indian Trail" leads through the grove way down here in the bowels of the earth, and as we emerge from its upper end we get our first glimpse of Taghanic Falls. Are you disappointed? True, there is not a great volume of water. But the fall, 215 feet, and the rocks rising 200 feet higher! In ages past that water fell on the spot on which we now stand. * Approach nearer, get alongside it, almost beneath it—now look up. Your disappointment vanishes like the thin, vapory mist thrown off by the water in its descent from the heights above. The volume of water is not great, but it floats, comes to you, gently as the dew drops, hiding the jagged rocks behind it in a light filmy veil. Sitting here in this great semi-circular ampitheatre, whose rocky walls tower 400 feet above us, with dado and frieze and cornice, the entablature surmounted by pines, the blue sky the dome, can you not liken your selves unto listeners in a grand cathedral to a sermon that mortal man cannot preach? From the center of the wall, over a triangular rock about 90 feet wide, the water flows in an unbroken sheet but a little ways, breaks into large, pearly drops, then turns into spray and falls into the pool below with less noise and tumult than is created by a summer shower. But imagine the roar in the spring and fall when the stream pouring over in great fury, causes even the windows and doors in the hotel 400 feet above, to rattle with a great noise, the precipice fairly trembling from the constantly recurring shocks of the heavy body of water falling this great height. With a feeling of awe and rest and contentment we quietly turn away and retrace our steps to the stone we had marked as being the entrance to the path down which we came, or leaped, and begin the ascent. If we could leap up the precipitous side of the hill as readily as we did down! It is hard work, but clinging to friendly bushes or leaning against convenient trees, and frequently resting, we finally arrive at the stairway. It is only 117 steps —you have ample opportunity to count them—to the top, then the balance of the ascent is easy; and with a cooling draught of water from the crystal spring bubbling forth from a little rustic arbor near the end of the path, we return to the hotel, sit down in a comfortable chair and anxiously await the call to dinner. There are other and easier routes by which the bottom of the gorge may be reached, but as this was the nearest, and our time is limited, it was chosen. Anyhow the exercise is beneficial, and gives you a better idea of your powers of endurance. Having dined, we light cigars and stroll over to the "lookout," built like a bird's nest among the limbs of a tree standing on the very edge of the abyss. Higher than the falls by 200 feet, we obtain a magnificent view of the

---

* "The Taghanic Falls * * have receded something more than a mile from the lake." "In its passage the stream first produced a series of falls and rapids, but finally receded so as to form a single fall. This is caused by the higher strata being so much harder than those below that a firm table is formed of these, while those below are undermined."—*Geol. IV Dist.*, p.p. 378-379.

TAGHANIC FALLS—215 FEET.

"bridal veil of Taghanic;" the gorge, with its vast walls—here the bare and treeless heights, there the densely wooded sides—and the lake. Like Niagara, Taghanic has had its "Blondin," but he achieved neither world-wide fame nor a hat full of money. In the month of September, 1874, "Professor" Jenkins shot a ball of twine across the gorge at this point; with the twine he drew over a heavy cord, then a rope and after considerable labor had stretched a cable of sufficient strength for his purposes. In emulation of the "fiends" at Niagara the north side of the gorge was boarded in by the proprietor of the hotel and an admission fee charged those desirous of witnessing the "Professor" disport on the rope from within this enclosure. The good people were not thus to be swindled; they flocked over to the south side, and the "Professor" exhibited his skill and daring on the slender thread suspended over this dizzy chasm for little more than the unremunerative local fame it gave him. But the attention of the public was drawn to the superior views obtained from the hitherto unfrequented south side, and as a result the Cataract House was built and has ever since remained the favorite resort of visitors.

Our excursion to the bottom of the gorge has left us without **sufficient ambition** to explore the beautiful upper ravine, but if you follow my advice **you will come** and spend a week or two at the Cataract House with Mr. Mockford. And your time will be fully occupied between gaining a further acquaintance **with the** gorge below and exploring the ravine above—going down to the top of the **fall**, climbing up into the eyrie clinging to the face of Eagle Cliff, or following the stream bed through **ravine and glen to pretty cascades beyond.** We return to **Ithaca** by the lower or lake **road.** The drive is made attractive by charming bits **of glen and** lake scenery, with numerous little waterfalls to **remind** us of that **one of greater beauty,** whose picture is so indelibly imprinted **on our memory.**

BUTTERMILK CREEK.

As Bohemians for the time being we can walk, and **the exercise we have taken has fitted us** for the perfect enjoyment **of a brisk walk of** two miles south along ths Newfield Road **to Buttermilk Creek. Starting early in the** morning, when the **sun is just beginning to peep over the hilltops, and** walking merrily along the base of the hill forming the eastern **boundary of the** Valley of the Inlet, we very unexpectedly come upon a mountain **torrent rushing** madly down the hillside and broken by its tumble over the rocky bed **into a mass of thick,** frothy foam. So unexpectedly had we come upon this **beautiful cascade that,** momentarily, **surprise** exceeds the pleasure, for **we are** totally unprepared for such a scene. **On the north, the** cultivated fields extend to the very edge of the sloping rockbed of the **torrent,** while on the south a dark forest entirely covers the hill, the "Buttermilk" **forming a** dividing line between the two extremes. At the foot lies our road, here **abruptly** turning to the right and following the westerly course of this stream, **which has** come rushing, tumbling down from a hundred and twenty-five or fifty **feet above.** This is but the first of a series of cascades, less in size but equal in beauty, that are hid from our gaze in the ravine, beginning at the head of the fall. The ascent **is quite easy, the bed of the fall** being so inclined that it presents a **series of small steps, and mounting, we stand on a level platform** at the top and just midway **between two falls—at the summit** of the first and almost at the foot of the second, **which is enclosed by rocky walls** rising far above it. Behind us the Valley of the Inlet, the "Forest City", **and the lake** bathed in the morning sun ; in front, the ravine, with its glittering cascades. We clamber up the side of the second fall, about 100 feet high, and soon reach a second plateau. The ravine widens **out, its** sides rise higher and higher, and we stand in a large ampitheatre which closes gradually around in front of us and is there broken by a narrow cleft extending down to within thirty feet of where we stand. There the rocks project in a semi-circular form, making a perfect "pulpit" or "stand", about forty feet wide, **the narrow gorge** that ends in it making a sudden turn a few yards back, and leaving, or seeming to **leave,** a niche in the rocks a yard or two in width, **from** which emerges the orator—the bright little stream—and standing but a moment in the pulpit, falls over in the streambed below. Climbing the steep hill on our right, we make a detour through the woods and returning to the ravine, clamber down its side and are again in the bed of the stream, but above Pulpit Falls, to the summit of which we return for a view of the valley whence we came, by the

RAVINE—BUTTERMILK CREEK.

narrow gorge through which the stream winds. The sides of the ravine overhead nearly touch, but widen out towards the bottom and are hollowed out in strange forms by the action of the water. The stream is but a few feet wide, rushing through a flume it has cut in the rocks, with several slight falls and with here and there a well or pocket worn in the rock by the whirling of a stone in the long ago. One of these wells is twelve feet in diameter and nine feet deep. You are inclined to spend more time in this "pass" than as your guide I can allow, hence I hurry you through and back to the ravine above, from whence, glancing up the stream, we see some of the most exquisite glen scenery in nature. The gorge is deep and narrow, the cascades curious and near together, the rocks picturesque and fantastic, the trees gracefully and charmingly grouped. Advancing, we pass one after another of the cascades, set in the lichened bank, with moss grown trees and curious rocks around them, and when we reach the fourth in this series the scene suddenly changes. The banks, losing their rocky steepness, slope gradually down to the water's edge, the stream glides along with but few interruptions of cascades in its easy descent, and grows more and more brooklike. Moss and ferns and evergreens are all around and quiet and peace are the characteristics. Then rounding a bend again the scene suddenly changes. Again the banks have risen until they tower an hundred feet above us, their sides bare and sombre and their bases nearly meeting ; the stream widens out to about fifty feet, and falls in a cascade of rare beauty some twenty or thirty feet, its width seemingly lessened by the projecting banks, behind which we catch glimpses of the widening stream above us. Just above the cascade, and in towards the bank, in bold relief against the dark rocks, rises a mass of stone, a pillar fringed with moss and ferns, rearing itself straight up fifty feet and tapering to a point crowned with vines and flowers. This is Steeple Rock, and the strata of rock that compose it project over each other so as to form a circular pathway to its summit, which may be reached by the expert climber. But first we must climb cautiously around the right hand bank of the stream on a ledge, seemingly cut out for our convenience, and rounding the projecting bank come in full view of the cascade, above which rises Steeple Rock. Then the stream winds through narrow rocky banks, the one side steep, grey, ragged and sombre in color ; the other sloping and wooded; there is but one cascade of any size above Steeple Rock, and we only too soon reach the bridge which marks the end of Buttermilk Ravine. Were we not Bohemians we would have a carriage meet us at this point, but the walk is not quite three miles back to Ithaca, the scenery varied and charming, with magnificent views of Ithaca and the lake, and forms a delightful ending to our day's pleasure. There remains yet one more excursion out of the village, and this to

ENFIELD FALLS.

For it we engage a carriage in the morning and drive south over the same road which led us to Buttermilk Creek. Pausing a moment at the foot of Buttermilk Falls, to again note this curious cascade and its strange surroundings, we then follow the road in its turnings for about a mile, when a guideboard instructs us to turn to the right and up the hill. Although the hill is long, it is covered with a dense wood of pine and hemlock, which, while shading us from the glare of the morning sun, presents many interesting features that serve to relieve the trip of tediousness. No sooner do we emerge from the woods and arrive at the top of the hill, with its view of the valley in the north and pine-clad hills, rising one above another in the south, than we begin the descent on the other side. About one-fourth of the way down, however, another signboard directs us to turn to the left, and we go down into a deep little valley, hollowed out here between the hills. At the foot of the hill is the "Enfield Falls Hotel," but you look around in vain for the falls or even any sign of them. Upon the side of the stable into which our horses are driven is nailed a small board, on which is painted, "Admission to the Falls, 10 cents," and in reply to our inquiry the bright little urchin that takes charge of the team says, "Down there they are," pointing to the rocky wall which apparently forms the eastern and an insurmountable boundary to the the valley. And to "down there" we then proceed, crossing on our way a noisy brook going in the same direction. As we near this rocky wall we observe a narrow "pass" into which the brook is entering. We also enter and are instantly transposed from the realms of commonplace into that of the picturesque. This "pass" is less than fifty feet wide and its bare grey walls rise to a height of nearly 200 feet. "The rock is of soft slate and shales, alternating with strata of harder sandstones, all lying nearly horizontal. The softer shales wear away, and the harder sandstones form numerous cascades, and also forms the bed of the ravine, which in places is nearly as level as a floor. The strata fracture in straight lines, and thus are formed walls and buttresses, marvellously regular, and adorned with frieze and cornice and battlement, as if some crazy architect had mingled half a dozen styles. Steps and walls and terraces are there; the narrow places have been widened by art and the way is easy and pleasant," The brook has left its gravelly bed amid the pastures green and its way henceforth is full of trouble. We pass down on the right side of the stream, which falls over its rocky bed in frequent cascades, and then rushes through a narrow channel like a flume, worn in the rocks. Crossing here by a little bridge, we descend a wide staircase cut in the rock into a sort of recess, with regular walls and a level rocky floor, alongside the stream. The ravine has grown deeper and wider, and the sides, which at first rose grey and bare and were then covered with trees and bushes, are now dark and naked. The stream leaves its narrow channel, at the end

ENFIELD RAVINE.

of which a well thirty feet deep and nine feet in diameter has been worn in the rocks, and also widens, but for a short distance only, and then making its way through a narrow Z shaped pass, falls a distance of about thirty feet in a beautiful foaming cascade. Passing along narrow rocky shelves and down rock staircases we follow the stream, and in a moment stand on the brink of the great Enfield Falls, 160 feet high. The scene has changed—in that part of the ravine through which we have passed we were impressed by its picturesque beauty; but here is granduer. Above the falls the scenes are pretty, interesting—below they are sublime, awe-inspiring. The fall is not perpendicular, but the water goes tumbling and rebounding down the rocks in masses of foam. A well made and safe path permits an easy descent to its base. First down a short staircase alongside the falling water, into which you can dip your hand as you descend, then on a shelf cut in the face of the rock, across a bridge built against the precipice and by a winding way among the trees—it is but a few moments until we stand at the foot of the falls and look up. The precipice rises 380 feet on either side, covered with lichens and ferns and crowned by the green boughs of hemlocks and pines. The water sparkles in the sunlight, changing from emerald into diamond drops and back again many times before falling into the dark pool at the base, and then winding its way through wood and glen, over little cataracts and into the Inlet two and a half miles below. There are many scenes of quiet beauty below the falls that would delight the soul of an artist, but they seem tame in comparison with the wild portion of the ravine through which we have come. We retrace our steps and as we return along the rock-hewn paths we are in perfect accord with the writer who has said: "Probably there is no ravine in the world which furnishes more variety in so short a space as that which extends from the rocky entrance so securely guarded by the granite champions, to the dizzy verge of the grand fall a few hundred yards below. Every foot of progress discloses some new and singular formation of rock entirely dissimilar from any preceding it. Cascades of every conceivable form and height, and deep, narrow channels which sometimes conceal in their rumbling depths the fiercely running water, follow each other in such rapid and agreeable succession that the spectator is at once lost in wonder and delight." We partake of a hearty dinner at the quaint little hotel, go down once more through the ravine to the great fall, and then are ready for the homeward drive and a brief visit to

LICK BROOK.

This wild but pretty mountain brook is seldom visited because of its inaccessibility and the number of other and equally or more attractive streams that are easier of access. The lover of solitude, however, will find in its wild beauty a charm that will enable him to look at all obstacles as being simply a presage to the finest enjoyment and will therefore willingly undergo the fatigue and discomfort attendant upon its exploration for the pleasure which follows. It is found in the woods about a mile south of Buttermilk Creek and is best reached from Ithaca by a drive of three miles along the Newfield road to the white Gothic cottage of Farmer Williams, where your team may be hitched and a walk of half a mile east brings you to the mouth of Lick Brook ravine. It is a half way point between the "Forest City" and Enfield Falls, and in returning from the latter place this white Gothic cottage, about half a mile off from our road, forms a landmark we cannot mistake. Hitching our horses then, at Farmer Williams' stable, we trudge across the meadows to the mouth of the brook and following the bed of the stream from the point where it empties into the Inlet, have gone but a little ways into the woods when our progress is barred by a precipice fifty feet in height over which is pouring or spraying the stream, the water being so widely distributed that it is barely sufficient to cover the green and mossy wall. Climbing out of this circular rocky basin we clamber up the north bank of the stream and attempt to follow a leaf-strewn path through the bushes and trees. Through a vista we see a second fall, similar in size and appearance to the first, but the difficulties in reaching it are so great that we do not care to overcome them, and continuing our rugged way soon discover a comparatively easy path that leads down into the ravine above this second fall, and are fully rewarded for our temerity. Shut in on one side by walls of solid rock, on the other by a steep wooded bank, with a gleam of sunlight through the leaves of the trees whose overhanging branches form an unique covering, the only sound the murmuring of the water, were you desirous of solitude here your wish would be in the fullest gratified. It is a retreat from the sorrows or the joys of this earth into which one can retire and commune with one's self and emerge the better for it. This part of the ravine is about one-fourth of a mile in length, ending at the second fall in the lower end and in a large amphitheatre at the upper. The walk through it is filled with pleasure, the moss-grown rocky walls, with here and there a crevice containing sufficient earth to afford nutriment for the ferns or shrubs clinging tenaciously there for life, the bright-colored foliage on the other side contrasting strongly with the dark

ITHACA AND ITS RESOURCES.   27

ENFIELD FALLS—160 FEET.

green on this, the babbling brook —all lending to the picturesque and beautiful effect produced in the scene. Down a rocky slope, lined on either side by the dark forest and into the amphitheatre, rushes the now angry brook, confined to narrow limits and apparently concentrating all its power for this supreme effort— a great fall from the heights 160 feet above. Differing in its surroundings from all the other falls in this region, this little torrent rushing down its steep rocky bed, although not so grand as some of the others, still has the power to attract even when our visits to Ithaca Gorge, Glenwood, Taghanic, Buttermilk and Enfield make comparison unfavorable, and we linger longer here than at some of the greater falls. Back through the ravine, and climbing out of its depths, we carefully seek the way to the foot of the hills, leaving the climb to the top of the great fall for some other time. Our team awaits us across the meadow, the drive of three miles to Ithaca is quickly accomplished and the ending of another day finds us with our admiration for the "Forest City" and its surroundings constantly increasing.

SIX MILE CREEK AND OTHER FALLS.

There are so many other glens and falls of lesser attractiveness, in comparison with those we have visited, but still worth seeing, that it is impossible at present to pay them all the attention they deserve. In Six Mile Creek, which forms the southern boundary of the village and winds around between the hills in the southeast, there are two very pretty cascades and attractive ravines, in exploring which we emerge at brief intervals into the sight of farm houses and cultivated fields. A delightful drive down the eastern shore of the lake will discover several beautiful glens, the most pleasing of which are "Burdick's" and McKinney's. Burdick's glen is directly opposite Glenwood and is only a few steps from the lake shore, but is concealed from passing boats by thick foliage. Its vast rocky amphitheatre and waterfall of 160 feet are very interesting. About half way between the "Corner of the Lake" and Burdick's are McKinney's glens, which may be visited on the way to or from the latter. A few rods north of Buttermilk Creek is Barnes's glen, the upper portion of which is very attractive, having huge rocks and several falls, one of them being over 100 feet high. But every day that is passed in this vicinity brings forth some new delight and surprise in the shape of glen, fall and ravine. "It is like a volume of weird and gloomy romance bound up in a gay library, and there is enjoyment in the quick contrast of the same morning in street and glen," said "Sentinel" in the New York *World* some ten years ago, and age has only made greater the contrast. With a brief visit to the beautiful Cascadilla and the Grounds of Cornell University I will then leave you to seek out the rest of these hidden joys for yourself, the assurance being mine that I will at least have your thanks for my feeble attempt to describe for you the sights that would afford you much pleasure.

CASCADILLA GLEN.

Less than five minutes walk from State, the principal business street, we step from the busy town directly into the deep, cool Cascadilla Glen, beginning at Williams' Mill, near the corner of Linn and Mill streets, and in the very centre of the village. At this same point it was, in fact, that the first settlers built their cabins, and thence the village grew out in a face-like shape. A neat iron bridge here spans the stream, which takes a northwesterly course through the village to the Inlet, and we pass around the mill, through the yard, and instantly find ourselves in a retired spot whence we more fully appreciate that "enjoyment in the quick contrast of the same morning (and almost the same instant) in street and glen." Here is a fall which, notwithstanding the abstraction of so much water from the stream above for the purposes of the mill, furnishes an interesting introduction to our ramble. Crossing the brook on stepping stones and keeping on the right hand side of the stream we presently turn a corner and are in a vast, solemn hall of nature. The stream turns two corners in instant succession, forming an amphitheatre at the bend which strikingly impresses us with the age and power of these floods in wearing away the solid rocks in such deep and graceful curves. Over the rocks and into the amphitheatre trickles the water that is permitted to escape from the dam above, but in time of freshet this double bend is the scene of mad, boiling and thunderous excitement as the floods go plunging through the tortuous bed. Here on account of its narrowing width the glen more properly becomes a ravine, and we are obliged to clamber up the north bank and walk along the brink of a precipice, but the glimpses of glen and stream below well repay us for the exertion. Then our way lies through a grove of pines and hemlocks, the path winds up and down along the hillside and we frequently stop with a shudder as the thought strikes us, "what if we were to make a misstep and go tumbling headlong into the depths

THIRD FALL, LICK BROOK—160 FEET.

of the ravine," this side of which is now a steep wooded bank and the opposite a frowning precipice. If you love the spice which danger gives you may go down into the stream bed, but it requires a steady hand and a cool head to make the descent by clinging to the bushes, and your hands and clothing will probably be fearfully torn before you reach the bottom. We follow the path until we come to the University bridge, where the descent is much easier, and we stand at the foot of the Giant's Staircase, and watch the water tumbling down as regular a flight of stairs as ever a boy fell down two steps a time. As far as the eye can see above are a series of pretty little cascades, closely enbosomed in rocky and arborescent banks. The ravine looks so very inviting that we climb the Giant's Staircase and picking our way along the bed of the stream, scaling the miniature cataracts, follow on until our progress is barred by an unromantic dam, when we return to the bridge over the Giant's Staircase by a pleasant shaded walk between the Cascadilla and an artificial brook leading to Willow Pond, the pretty terraced reservoir from which is drawn the water supply for the Cascadilla Building owned by Cornell University and occupied as a dormitory for students. From the bridge 70 feet above the stream, is obtained a most comprehensive view of the Cascadilla and its numerous cascades, and through a vista in the evergreens almost meeting in a pointed arch over the stream, the village appears in the distance. Were it not for the massive Cascadilla Building so close on the south bank of the stream, the terrace and the fine University roadway, we could readily imagine ourselves in a wilderness, but one from which a stone could be thrown into the midst of a city and civilization. But let us take only a few steps north and the wild and the picturesque is lost in the highest type of cultivation. We have entered the domains of Cornell University.

CORNELL UNIVERSITY.

Here upon this gradually sloping plateau, over three hundred feet above the level of Cayuga Lake, with the famous Ithaca Gorge for its northern and the beautiful Cascadilla for its southern boundary, stand the buildings of this noble institution "where any person can find instruction in any study." Winding drives and walks and terraces and lawns make attractive the surroundings from which nothing is detracted by the numerous buildings. Those which stand out most prominently are the Armory and Gymnasium, a brick building, with stone trimmings, and Romanesque in style, which is situated nearest the Cascadilla; the Sage College, a handsome brick building in the Italian Gothic style of architecture, which stands on a knoll a little northeast of the Armory; the Sage Chapel; the Morrill and White Halls and the Mc Graw building, with its massive tower, over 120 feet high and containing the chime of bells—this group being an adaptation of the renaissance and built of dark blue stone with light trimmings; the new Chemical and Physical Laboratory; the Sibley College of Mechanic Arts and the old laboratory and machine shops. Scattered about are the homes of the faculty, on a knoll in the rear is the elegant house of the President, and back of all the great college farm. With magnificent views of lake and valley, with on either side ravines and rocks and waterfalls, the site is unequaled and Cornell University should be the pride of the great Empire State.

Fifteen years ago there was nothing on this hill save an unkempt cornfield, difficult of access, marred by rail fences, gashed by ravines, and utterly unfit, to all appearances, for any use by a seminary of learning. Behold the transformation! This rough hill has been wrought into a verdant slope, its disadvantages transformed into beauties; where was then an unkempt cornfield are now lawns and terraces of great beauty; where was then but marring rail fences are now these grand edifices, so imposing in architectural design and proportions. From every land has been gathered a wealth of apparatus and collections illustrative of science, art and industry probably second to none in the country; a library third in importance among the University libraries of the whole land, and rapidly becoming the equal of the first; and the largest and most completely equipped laboratories erected yet built in this country—a University established that has already been acknowledged to have but three rivals in the land. Truly, here "a great work has been done; a great work is doing; a great work is evidently to be done."

* * * * * * * * * *

When, in 1862, the bill presented by Hon. Justin S. Morrill, United States Senator from Vermont, "having as its purpose to create and maintain colleges in the various States, having as their object instruction in the sciences applicable to the great industries of the country, including military instruction, and not excluding instruction in science and literature in general," appropriated to each State landscrip covering 30,000 acres of land for each representative of a State in Congress, the question arose with the Legislatures of the different States as to what should be done with it. Some appropriated it to existing colleges for the purpose of founding scientific and technical schools ; others founded new institutions. New York having thirty-three representatives, her share was 990,000

McGraw-Fiske Mansion. Sage Chapel. Morrill Hall. McGraw Building. White Hall. Chemical and Physical Laboratory. Sibley Building.
CORNELL UNIVERSITY CAMPUS—LOOKING NORTHWEST FROM SAGE COLLEGE.

acres, but the course taken by her Legislature was at first unfortunate, the whole grant being appropriated to an institution known as the "People's College"—established at the upper end of Seneca Lake—on very easy conditions. For two years that institution held the grant, but did nothing toward accomplishing the conditions, and finally allowed it to lapse and return to the State, rather than take any further trouble in the matter.

Among the new members of the Legislature which came together in 1864, were Ezra Cornell, of Ithaca, and Andrew D. White, of Syracuse. Shortly after the beginning of the session Mr. White was made Chairman of the Committee on Public Instruction. Almost the first measure which came before that committee was a bill to incorporate the public library of Ithaca, to which Mr. Cornell proposed to give $100,000. On looking into the charter as he proposed it, Mr. White was struck by its breadth and liberality. There were no petty limitations of any sort—no conditions as to creed or party in the controlling board. This led to an acquaintance between the two men to whom the institution of which I am telling you—Cornell University—owes its being, an acquaintance which ripened into friendship. Every day they talked over some subject connected with the proposed library, and with the educational needs of the country. In the meantime the question had again come up as to what the State should do with the educational land grants. The "People's College" authorities, it was now evident, would do nothing with it, and as this was generally seen there was a rush upon the Legislature by the authorities of nearly all the other colleges in the State —over twenty in number—and especially by the promoters of the new State Agricultural College, which had been established at Ovid. The various college authorities demanded that the whole sum arising from the sale of the land scrip should be divided up between them in equal parts. As the whole sum likely to be realized from this source was estimated officially by the Comptroller at $600,000, it was evident that in this case each institution would receive between $20,000 and $30,000—hardly more than one-half enough for the establishment of a single professorship. Mr. Cornell and his associated trustees of the Agricultural College sought to divide the fund into two parts—one-half to remain with the "People's College" and the other half to be appropriated to the State Agricultural College. The contest became very animated.

Against all these efforts to divide the fund Mr. White took a firm stand, both in the Senate and in the committee. His ground was that it was an opportunity almost providential for the establishment of a university on a large scale, and with provisions for modern scientific and technical instruction in the State of New York; that this might be done if the fund were kept together somewhere; that the chance would be lost and the various small denominational colleges only slightly strengthened if the same were divided. To see such a university established in the State in which he was born had been Mr. White's dream for years. Even while a member of one of the smaller denominational colleges in the State, and before going to a New England university, he had thought much over the needs of the State in this respect. Afterwards as a student at Yale College, and still later at the College of France in Paris, and at the University of Berlin, the same question was constantly present with him. On his return from a three years' study abroad, his first effort was to enlist strong men in the establishment of a real university as distinguished from the denominational colleges. He laid plans before the late Gerrit Smith, who gave close attention to them, and at the time seriously thought of making a great endowment. Mr. White offered, if he would establish such an institution in the central part of the State of New York, to add to it the half of his own fortune. He also talked and corresponded with George Wm. Curtis, who showed much interest in this, as in every other good cause. But as no definite work seemed likely to be begun, he accepted an invitation to the Professorship of History in the University of Michigan, seeing there the only chance to aid in laying the foundation of a true university. After four years of work there, he was elected very unexpectedly to the Senate of New York, where he met for the first time, Ezra Cornell.

The struggle regarding the disposal of the fund became more and more bitter. But Mr. White steadily took the ground that while the rule for primary education is diffusion of resources, the rule for advanced education is concentration of resources. Thanks to the good sense of the Committee on Education, this view prevailed, and although the Legislature was deluged with petitions from the districts where the various sectarian colleges were situated, all these tendencies to scatter the fund were resisted. While this struggle was going on, Mr. Cornell one day met Mr. White on his way from the State House, at Albany, and seemed to have something on his mind. At last he said: "I have five hundred thousand dollars more than my family need. I would like to do something with it for the benefit of the State, and I would like your advice regarding it." Mr. White answered: "Mr. Cornell, the most important things to be taken care of in this State, of course, are the charities and the common school education. But you can rely on the hearts of the whole people to take care of the charities. They will see to it that human suffering is alleviated. As to common school education, you can rely upon the State to take charge of that. But the advanced and higher instruction, without which common school education will always be weak and poor, and without which our civilization will be of a very low order, must be taken care of by the comparatively few men who see the importance of it. In my judgment, if you have such a sum to give, it can best be given to promote advanced education in science, literature and the arts for the benefit of the State and Nation." Mr. Cornell thanked him and there the subject ended for the time.

During the summer after the close of the Legislature, Mr. White was invited by the trustees of the State Agricultural College, and by Mr. Cornell, to meet them at Rochester. He did so, and Mr. Cornell then laid before them a definite proposal. He said that Mr. White's arguments as to the necessity of a very large sum being required to found an institution for advanced instruction had converted him; that he was prepared to meet that view, and he proposed that if the State would accept his proposal to divide the fund into two parts, leaving half where it already was—with the "People's College"—and giving the other half to the Agricultural College at Ovid, he would give to the latter institution $300,000; thus enabling it to have as large an endowment as if the entire land grant had been given it, since that was estimated by the Comptroller at $500,000. The trustees, including a large number of the most prominent men in the State, were greatly delighted with this, expressing their opinions most favorably. But on being asked for his view, Mr. White declared that he would oppose any such measure; that he would stand firm against any division of the land grant whatever. An expression of disappointment and even of disgust was general in the meeting, but Mr. White kept on and stated that it was clear to him that the "People's College" would do nothing, and that if Mr. Cornell would ask in behalf of his institution for the whole fund, and give to the State the $300,000 as proposed, he would support the measure. Nothing more was said at the time, but some time afterward Mr. Cornell, in the same quiet, firm manner came forward and made another proposal. Both he and Mr. White had satisfied themselves that the State Agricultural College had no future—it was, in fact, already a failure and had been closed for lack of students. Mr. Cornell's proposal now was that if the State would establish a new institution at Ithaca, N. Y., he would give to it $500,000. At the next session of the Legislature a bill was introduced in accordance with Mr. Cornell's proposal. As to the name of the institution, he had never expressed any wish; his intention was simply that it should receive the title of Ithaca State College or something similar. But at Mr. White's urgent request he consented that it should bear the name of Cornell University, his view being that this was not only due Mr. Cornell, but was strictly in accordance with the best American precedents.

The bill for the new University was very carefully drawn, the main hand in the work besides Mr. Cornell's and Mr. White's being that of Senator Charles J. Folger, Chairman of the Judiciary Committee, and since that time Chief Justice of the State of New York and Secretary of the United States Treasury. The main features of the bill were that it proposed the establishment of a real university, enabling the funds provided by Mr. Cornell to be used in establishing such departments and courses of study in addition to those named in the original act of Congress, as might be necessary to give the institution a university character. Now began a struggle both in the Committees of the Upper and Lower Houses, and in open Senate and Assembly. The bill was fought fiercely at every stage of its progress. All tactics possible were resorted to in order to delay or destroy it. Political influences, influences of great corporations, were arrayed against it. The Legislature was flooded with petitions from the localities where the various denominational colleges were situated, and every denomination was strongly represented among the opponents. The measure was called by various opprobrious names. Mr. Cornell was called a "land-grabber," a "land-thief"—was charged with wishing to "erect a monument to himself." The project was spoken of as "Utopian," "visionary," "crack-brained," "godless." In order to meet this opposition Mr. Cornell, at the request of Mr. White, invited small bodies of Senators and Assemblymen to his room to hear Mr. White present his views as to the measure and as to the character of the bill. In this way strength was steadily gained. Such Senators as Mr. Andrews, then of Herkimer County; Havens, of Essex; Folger, of Ontario; Allen, of Chautauqua; and such Assemblymen as Henry B. Lord, of Tompkins; Daniel P. Wood, of Onondaga, and others, became its firm friends, standing from first to last in favor of the Cornell University bill against political pressure, appeals of the sectarian colleges and the clamors of various localities. Thanks also to Horace Greeley, Erastus Brooks, George William Curtis and Manton Marble, Mr. White was enabled to meet the various

A VIEW OF THE UNIVERSITY AT AN EARLIER PERIOD.
The North, South and McGraw University Buildings (then so-called, and the principal buildings first erected).

attacks in the New York papers. At times the measure appeared to be hopelessly lost. After a severe struggle it passed the Senate, but having got into the Education Committee of the Assembly it remained there, and no arguments were able to induce the committee to report. From some cause, which has never been cleared up, that committee refused week after week, month after month, to present the bill to the Assembly even for consideration. Finally the friends of the measure rallied in force, took the bill out of the hands of the committee and brought it to a consideration by the two-thirds vote required for such action. Then the contest thickened—leading men were summoned from various parts of the country to work against it; some of the most active legislative agents of corporations, and some of the most skillful wire pullers, exerted themselves to the utmost to defeat the measure, but all in vain. The bill finally passed the Assembly, but it was amended. And here came new complications and troubles. While the bill was yet in the Senate the friends of one of the smaller denominational colleges in the State came in force to the Legislature to oppose the measure. They declared their college had never received anything from the State and that it must now have something. Among other things, it was proposed that Mr. Cornell should pledge himself, in case the bill passed, to give $25,000 to found a professorship in the college referred to. There were not wanting men who advised Mr. Cornell to accept these terms, but his answer was in accordance with his manly, straightforward, honest nature. He said: "Never! I will make no pledges or promises in private. Whatever you can induce the Legislature to put into the bill, I will consider—I will accept or reject it, but it must be open so that all men can see and understand the whole transaction." The result was that a clause was inserted in the bill in the Assembly making it a condition of the establishment of the new university that $25,000 should be given by Mr. Cornell for founding a professorship in agricultural chemistry in Genesee College; in other words, before Mr. Cornell could be allowed to give $500,000 to the State, he must give $25,000 to a Methodist College. When the bill came back to the Senate with this amendment another storm arose, but in view of the approaching end of the session and the necessity of coming to some conclusion, the bill was passed as amended and became a law.

But there was still another rock on which the new enterprise might split. The bill contained a proviso that the trustees of the "People's College" might retain the land grant, should they comply with such conditions as the Regents of the State University might declare equivalent to a compliance with the conditions imposed upon the States when the land grant was first turned over to them. The regents fixed the sum at $150,000, and three months was allowed for them to obtain this sum. The trustees of the "People's College" gave no sign, allowed the whole three months to elapse, did nothing and so lost the grant. And now Mr. Cornell came forward, paid the $25,000 to the Genesee College, transferred not only the $500,000 originally required by the bill, but 200 acres of land in the town of Ithaca on which the University should be established, and it might also here be mentioned that he afterward gave sums out of his own fortune, running up his original gift to an aggregate little short of $1,000,000. Yet this was but a small part of the endowment due to him. With that wonderful foresight to which he owed his own fortune, he saw that a very large sum could be realized by the institution through the "location" of the land scrip received from the State. He was the only man in the United States who foresaw this and acted upon it. And hence arose the noblest endowment ever due for any purpose on this earth to a single individual.

The land which the general Government gave to each of the States, in the proportion of 30,000 acres to each representative in Congress, was represented by land scrip—that is, each State received land scrip for as many acres as it was entitled to under the act of 1862. The various States, anxious to realize money, threw this scrip representing Government land into the market. The result was that the market was soon glutted and the price of the scrip went down to a very low figure. Some of the States sold their scrip as low as 30 cents an acre. The Comptroller of the State of New York, when Mr. Cornell took up the matter, had already sold some of the scrip at about 60 cents. Mr. Cornell set himself to stop this as far as the State of New York was concerned. He determined to locate the "scrip"—that is, not to sell it, but to take up government lands with it. But the difficulty was that a State could not do this. The United States laws of 1862, which gave the land scrip, specially declared that no State should take up land within the boundaries of another State. There was an evident fear of an *imperium in imperio*. Seeing this Mr. Cornell came forward and offered to put himself under heavy bonds to "locate" the scrip for the benefit of Cornell University, paying, by a process carefully specified, the market value of the scrip into the State Treasury. After some opposition a law was passed to this effect, and Mr. Cornell devoted himself, in the midst of great business cares of his own, to obtaining with the scrip valuable pine lands in Wisconsin and farm lands in other States. In this he was indefatigable, visiting the most distant Western States, traveling night and day through the woods, selecting lands to the best advantage for the future University and devoting his own fortune to paying taxes, with the other enormous expenses attendant upon so large a transaction. Thus it was that he "located" about half a million acres, and with great care.

The bill passed by the Legislature regarding the Cornell University required it to be in operation by the 8th day of October, 1868. The delay of the "People's College" authorities in announcing their decision had held back the Cornell University, but at the first moment the trustees were brought together at Ithaca. At Mr. Cornell's request, Mr. White had drawn up a report on the organization of the University. This was read to the trustees, and as a result Mr. White was chosen President. Nothing was further from his expectations or wishes. He had business cares which seemed to attach him closely to the place where his family lived, Syracuse, N. Y. He was also greatly attached to his duties in the State Senate, and his work as Professor in the University of Michigan. Important business cares were upon him, and he had just been elected to a professorship at Yale College, which, if he returned to professional life, was just what he wished to take. But the earnestness of Mr. Cornell, the importance of making a proper beginning, led him to accept the Presidency of the new University as a temporary matter. He had no idea of remaining in it for more than a few months. His purpose was, in the meantime, to get the new enterprise started, and to aid in selecting a man who should carry it on. Shortly after, at the request of Mr. Cornell, the buildings having been begun and some professors called, President White was asked to go to Europe in order to study the organization of various technical institutions, to secure some professors and to purchase books and apparatus. With this request he complied, travelling through

England, France and Germany, looking closely at agricultural and technical schools and making large purchases of illustrative material and books of all sorts. Besides this he had the good fortune to interest and secure Mr. Goldwin Smith, then Professor of History at the University of Oxford, and highly esteemed on both sides of the Atlantic, for the Department of English History, and Dr. James Law, already an authority in veterinary science at the London College, for the College of Agriculture.

At the time required by the charter the University was open. There were very great difficulties—but two buildings were ready, and these were incomplete. There were no doors upon the student's rooms, no bridges across the streams and ravines—in fact, the difficulties were distressing. The interest in the new institution was great, however, and from all parts of the State people flocked in to the opening exercises. Although all went well, there were signs not at all pleasing. From all the denominational colleges and their supporters in the pulpit and in the sectarian press, began to come mutterings. The first sign was when the simple exercises at the opening of the University were attacked by a religious paper, so-called, most vehemently. Then it was that Mr. Cornell, President White and their associates saw what they had to face, for no campaign, even in the bitterness of a political contest, was ever more skillful for perverting and even falsifying fact than were some of the sectarian papers at that time. Every utterance was twisted from its true meaning. Words were put into the mouths both of Mr. Cornell and President White which they never dreamed of uttering. From various pulpits and papers went out the declaration that the new institution, being unsectarian, must needs be godless, atheistic, materialistic. The simple fact was, that the various colleges of the State, founded by different denominations, became alarmed at the number of students flocking to the new institution. Moreover, the older colleges had their graduates as teachers and professors in most of the academies and high schools in the State, and these made common cause with the colleges from which they came and the religious organizations to which they belonged. Their hostility, too, was increased by the the fact that the new institution, while it made ample provision for classical studies, also made more full provision than had heretofore been made in the interior of the State, for scientific and technical studies. This was at once regarded as an attack on classical studies, and any one connected with any preparatory school where a little Latin and less Greek were taught, came to look upon the new University as an enemy.

The charter of the University from the State had declared that persons of any religious and persons of no religious sect shall be equally eligible to all offices and appointments, but it had also declared regarding the governing body that a majority of the trustees should not be of any one religious sect. This clause would certainly seem to erect a complete barrier against religious control. At the worst, the institution was on the same footing with the public school system of the State. All such appeals were in vain, the war upon the University grew more and more bitter. But students came in spite of this, and in large numbers, and the work went on. A large faculty was gradually brought together, mainly graduates of the New England colleges who had supplemented their studies at

European Universities. Illustrative material of all sorts was increased. Mr. Cornell added to his previous gifts various large collections in Natural History; and other friends came forward to help. It was indeed, one of the most interesting results of the war waged by various denominational institutions and journals

THE SAGE COLLEGE FOR WOMEN.

and pulpits upon the institution that so many wealthy men attached to the same denominations came forward and contributed large sums to the institution. Mr. John McGraw, of Ithaca, gave $120,000 to erect a building for the Natural History collections and lecture rooms. Mr. Hiram Sibley gave then and afterwards about $100,000 for building, equipment and endowment for the Department of Mechanical Engineering. Mr. E. B. Morgan, of Aurora, gave a considerable sum for scientific expeditions to Brazil, headed by one of the University professors, of which a leading object was to add to the University collection in Natural History. Goldwin Smith gave his library in English History and Law, and a large sum of money in addition. Mr. Dean Sage gave $30,000 for the endowment of the University pulpit, thus providing for two sermons each Sunday from the most eminent divines of the several Christian denominations, throughout the Fall and Spring terms of the University year. Mr. Henry W. Sage gave something over $340,000 for a College for Women, and for other purposes. Mr. William Kelly gave $4,000 for a Mathematical Library, and President White gave over a hundred thousand dollars for various purposes of the institution. Mr. W. H. Sage gave $3,500 for a specific purpose, and various other individuals gave sums, large and small, for different purposes. The attacks on the University then, while they doubtless kept many young men from its privileges by false statements, arousing prejudice, really stirred the friends of the institution to greater endeavors than they would ever have made otherwise.

There were other difficulties to meet, however. The number of names presented for positions in the faculty of the institution was enormous; and many of the disappointed candidates and their friends were intensely disgusted at the short-sightedness of an institution which failed to recognize their claims. Multitudes of the people who infest and amuse American society were also greatly disappointed that their crotchets were not attached to the University, and henceforth many of them devoted themselves to showing that it could not possibly succeed. All these attacks seemed but to stimulate the friends of the institution to new exertions. Then came another class. It began to be seen that the amount to be realized from the "location" of the lands would be very large. Sundry journals and persons, partly from local jealousy, partly stirred by denominational influence, partly yielding to a wish to make a sensation by attacking a man so honest as Ezra Cornell, began to present him to the State as a man whose only purpose was to make a great fortune for himself out of the land. They called him "land thief" and "land grabber". At first Mr. Cornell prepared careful statements showing the falsity of these charges. They produced no effect whatever. These papers only redoubled their fury, reiterating the charges, inventing new statements in place of those which Mr. Cornell had exploded. At last this series of attacks was brought to a head through an onslaught made in the Legislature of the State by a member of that body from the district which had hoped to have the endowment, but through its own want of public spirit had lost it. In his speech the honorable gentleman berated Mr. Cornell at great length before the State as simply actuated by selfish motives and perpetrating a gigantic fraud on the State —in fact, as nothing more or less than a criminal who ought to be brought to justice. Mr. Cornell had been born in the State and had lived in it sixty years. He was known from one end of it to the other as a man of the noblest and purest character. All made no difference. The speech against him was printed at length in the leading papers of the State, and he was called upon to explain. He took all these attacks in the most quiet, philosophical way. When President White lamented them to him, he simply said that he rejoiced that they had come now instead of after his death; that now he was able to answer them. He immediately telegraphed and wrote to General Dix, then Governor of the State, requesting him to appoint a committee to investigate his acts, and that such committee should have in it a majority of men opposed to him politically. A committee was appointed composed of Horatio Seymour, John D. Van Buren and William A. Wheeler—three names honored throughout the entire State. The investigation made by them was most thorough. Its result was a complete vindication of Mr. Cornell in every particular ; and not only vindication but commendation of a very high sort, which coming as it did from a committee in which two of the members were politically opposed to Mr. Cornell, carried great weight. The truth of history must be mentioned, however, that, although the opinion of all thoughtful men was turned in Mr. Cornell's favor by these same journals, and although the member of the Assembly who made this most bitter attack virtually retracted his statements, one leading newspaper in the State, which was in the interest of a denominational college, persisted in reiterating the charges until Mr. Cornell's death.

* * * * * * * * * *

Despite the attacks continually made upon it, Cornell University throve and steadily advanced towards the objective point—a real university. When the institution was organized, its trustees thought it their duty under the charter to establish not only certain general, classical, scientific, philosophical, but certain special courses having reference to the development of the great industries of the country. All was experiment. No one knew how many would wish to take these courses. It was thought best to set the standard low at first, and gradually to raise it. In the first years neither algebra nor geometry was required—the result was that students were largely drawn from the upper classes of the high schools and the first year of its courses duplicated high-school work. This was found to be unjust to the schools, and to the industrial as well as the educational interests of the State. Then the standard was gradually raised, and has continued to be steadily raised, making the examinations more and more careful, down to the present time. For a time there was a considerable falling off, but the tide has turned and an upward movement has begun—Cornell University is no longer a dream, but a fact. Never were its circumstances more favorable, never were its prospects so satisfactory as now; the faith of its President has been justified; his promises more than fulfilled; and that his prophecy, "the progress of the next five years is to outstrip by far what has been done in the past ten," will be as fully realized, no person of an unprejudiced mind has the least doubt.

Upon the 265 acres comprising the University grounds have been erected sixteen University buildings, varying in cost from $3,000 to over $150,000. Of these sixteen buildings, the cost of four, and half the cost of another, has been borne by the University, leaving eleven and one-half as the gifts of individuals, and among these gifts are the two most expensive of all, to both of which have been added sums more than sufficient to maintain them in good repair. The appended table will show the cost of these buildings and the year in which erected:

BUILDING	YEAR	COST
1. Cascadilla Place	1868	$37,010.94
2. Morrill Hall	1868	70,111.25
3. McGraw Natural History Building	1871	120,000.00
4. Sibley College of Mechanic Arts	1871	28,821.14
5. President's House	1871	50,000.00
6. White Hall	1873	80,485.16
7. Old Laboratory	1873	23,699.12
8. South Farm Building	1873	5,000.00
9. Sage Chapel	1874	30,000.00
10. Sage College	1875	150,000.00
11. North Farm Building	1879	6,000.00
12. Botanical Laboratory and Greenhouses	1882	15,000.00
13. Sibley Foundry	1882	3,000.00
14. New Laboratory	1883	90,000.00
15. Armory and Gymnasium	1883	32,000.00
16. Memorial Chapel	1883	20,000.00
Total cost of Buildings		$761,127.61
Farm and Grounds		99,093.91
Total		$860,221.52

In the year 1881 Mrs Jennie McGraw Fiske bequeathed to the University $50,000 for the maintenance of the McGraw Natural History building, given by her father; $40,000 for the erection and maintenance of a Cottage Hospital for students, and the residue of her estate, amounting to nearly a million of dollars, to the University Library. Included in this residue was the beautiful house erected for her own residence on grounds adjoining the University Campus. But the legality of these bequests has been contested, and the matter is at present under litigation. Had the McGraw-Fiske mansion been included in the above list of buildings, it would have swelled the total by $210,000. In addition to the cost of buildings and grounds, the total cost, of the equipment of departments up to the present time is about $350,000, so that on the permanent equipment in the form of buildings, grounds, farm, library, machinery and apparatus and illustrative collections, all in constant use for purposes of instruction, there has been expended up to this time over twelve hundred thousand dollars; and a very large share of this sum has come from the private gifts of public-spirited citizens. During the past two years alone the following additions have been made: (1) A large addition to the botanical laboratories and conservatories—the gifts of Hon. Henry W. Sage—at a cost of $15,000. (2) The building for the use of the departments of chemistry and physics—the largest and best equipped thus far erected in the United States—at a cost of $90,000. (3) The armory and gymnasium, 60x160 feet and 30 feet high, with a wing containing baths, dressing rooms, etc., at a cost of $32,000. This gymnasium is under the charge of an experienced physician and gymnast, and physical training has the same careful attention as mental training. (4) An addition to the Sibley College of Mechanic Arts—the gift of Hon. Hiram Sibley—for the practical instruction of mechanical engineers in foundry work, at a cost of $3,000. (5) A special collection of models of mechanical movements, being duplicates of the celebrated Reuleaux collection of kinematic models made for the Imperial College of Mechanical Engineering at Berlin—also gift the of Mr. Sibley at a cost of $8,000. (6) A collection of instruments,

THE NEW CHEMICAL AND PHYSICAL LABORATORY.

photographs and models of bridges, roofs, railway plants, locks for slack water navigation, etc., for the use of the department of Civil Engineering, from Paris and Vienna, at a cost of over $10,000. (7) Very large additions to the chemical and physical apparatus, at a cost of $23,000. (8) Considerable additions to the Museum of Natural History, at a cost of $10,000. (9) Sundry additions to the Library, at a cost of about $35,000. (10) The residence and grounds of the late Mrs. Jennie McGraw-Fiske, being part of the residuary interest of her estate, together with the paintings, statuary, bronzes, tapestries and the extensive collection of examples of art as applied to industry, which at present form an art museum. The cost of the building, with its contents and grounds, as already stated exceeds $200,000. (11) The McGraw-Fiske Hospital for students, provided for in Mrs. Fiske's will by a bequest of $40,000. (12) A memorial chapel and mausoleum in honor of John McGraw, Mrs. Jennie McGraw-Fiske and Ezra Cornell, on the University grounds, by the trustees of the University and the executors of the estate of John McGraw and Mrs. Fiske, at a cost of $20,000. The liberality of the benefactors who have from time to time endowed the University renders it almost independent of students' fees, and but one-twentieth of all its revenue comes from this source. At the same time, the advantages it enjoys in buildings, equipments, etc., are unsurpassed by any, and equalled by few of the colleges of the country.

Cornell University differs from most educational institutions in the United States in (1) the addition to the ordinary governing faculty of non-resident professors and lecturers, some of whom deliver each year courses of lectures upon subjects in the investigation of which they have acquired a high reputation.; (2) liberty in the choice of studies ; (3) the prominence given to studies of practical utility ; (4) the absence of a marking system determining the relative rank of each student in his class ; (5) the non-sectarian character of the institution. The University is controlled by a board of trustees of twenty-three members, among them being the eldest male lineal descendant of the founder, together with the President of the University, the **Governor and** Lieutenant-Governor of the State, the **Speaker of the Assembly,** the Superintendent of **Public** Instruction, the President of **the State Agricultural Society and** the **Librarian of the Cornell** Library. Of **the remaining fifteen, two are** elected **annually** by **the trustees and one** by **the** Alumni, the term **of office** being five years.

The faculty now consists of forty-two resident **professors,** four non resident professors and lecturers, and eight instructors. **The work is** divided among twenty two departments, viz: Agriculture, entomology, veterinary science, mechanical engineering, military science, architecture, civil engineering, freehand drawing, mathematics and astronomy, physics, chemistry and mineralogy, botany, geology and palæontology, zoology (including human anatomy and hygiene and comparative anatomy), ancient classical languages, Oriental languages, Germanic languages, Romance languages. Anglo-Saxon and English literature, general literature and oratory, moral and intellectual philosophy, history and political science. The student has a choice between eighteen courses of study, of which seventeen lead to degrees, viz : Agriculture, mechanical engineering (two), architecture, civil engineering (two), electrical engineering. mathematics, chemistry and physics, analytical chemistry, natural history, medical preparatory, history and political science, arts, literature, philosophy, science, science and letters

For purposes of advanced study, the University extends its privileges to its own graduates, and to graduates of like standing from other colleges and universities, and it confers advanced degrees as below ; but graduate students who are not candidates for a degree are received in any department and for any length of time. To graduate students there is no charge for tuition, and they have the free use of the library, laboratories, and collections. In addition to the special courses of instruction given to undergraduates, courses of study for graduates leading to advanced degrees are provided for in the following general departments : History and Political Science, Philosophy and Letters, Comparative Philology, the Ancient Classical Languages and Literatures, the Oriental Languages and Literatures, the Modern European Languages and Literatures, Chemistry and Physics, Civil Engineering, Mechanical Engineering, Mathematics, Natural History ; and the following advanced degrees are offered : Master of Arts, Doctor of Philosophy, Civil Engineer, Mechanical Engineer, Master of Science, Doctor of Science, Doctor of Veterinary Medicine.

The Library now contains about forty-six thousand bound volumes, and fourteen thousand **pamphlets. It is a** working library, eminently adapted to the purposes of research, and especially rich in works on history, the ancient classical languages and literatures, the oriental languages and literatures, comparative philology, mathematics, agriculture, architecture, civil engineering and mechanical engineering. By the will of the late Mrs Jenny McGraw Fiske, who died in October, 1881, the Library received a specific bequest, and was also made residu-

SAGE CHAPEL - CORNELL UNIVERSITY, ITHACA, N.Y.

ary legatee. From this source there has been paid to the University, up to the present time, about $700,000; and the income from this fund, known as the McGraw Library Fund, is to be applied to the support and increase of the Library. Such courses as embody agriculture, mechanics, engineering, electrical engineering, agricultural chemistry and analytical chemistry are taught both practically and theoretically, and for this purpose the University has its farm, with model dairy, stock, etc.; its machine shops, and complete engineering department, equipped with the latest and best mechanical tools, machines and appliances; its chemical laboratory, where such work is performed as has special reference to the requirements of manufacturers; and an electrical department, furnished with a most complete set of electrical apparatus and appliances and especially arranged for instruction and experimental work. The extensive illustrative collections made for the working laboratories in the departments of chemistry, physics, botany, entomology, geology, palæontology, zoology, architecture, civil, mechanical and electrical engineering and veterinary science afford students every facility for thorough and comprehensive study and the University is continually increasing the facilities in these as well as in every other department.

By an act of the trustees passed in April, 1872, women are admitted to the University on the same terms as men, except that they must be seventeen years old. The elegant Sage College building was built, furnished and endowed by the Hon. Henry W. Sage as a place of residence for lady students, with the stipulation that "instruction should be afforded to young women by Cornell University as broad and thorough as to young men." The terms and conditions of admission to the University are that male candidates must be at least sixteen and female candidates seventeen years of age and must pass a thoroughly satisfactory examination. State students to the number of 128 may be admitted each year, the original act of incorporation providing for the admission of one student annually from each assembly district without payment of tuition. They are selected by competitive examinations from the various public schools and academies throughout the State. For State students, for students in agriculture and for all resident graduates pursuing post-graduate courses there is no charge for tuition or for the use of the library and the collections. Some of the students are enabled to support themselves wholly or in part, while pursuing their studies, by laboring on the farm, in the machine shop or in the printing establishment, for which they receive the usual rate of wages. It is also probable that at an early day a number of scholarships and fellowships will be established, according to the provision made in 1873 by the five trustees who who then gave to the University $150,000 to assist it out of financial difficulties.

The whole number of students that entered Cornell University in 1882, was 354, as against 408 in 1883—an increase of 54. The whole number of freshmen entering in 1882, was 137, as against 165 in 1883—an increase of 28. This is an excellent showing, of which the citizens of Ithaca, equally with the University authorities, feel a justifiable pride.

The University, established by a government which recognizes no distinction of religious belief, seeks neither to promote any creed nor to exclude any. By the terms of its charter, persons of any religious denomination or of no religious denomination are equally eligible to all offices and appointments, and it is expressly ordered that "at no time shall a majority of the board of trustees be of any one religious sect, or of no religious sect"; but, though it cannot be sectarian, it is not unchristian. In the University Chapel religious services are held, and discourses delivered by eminent clergymen of the various Christian denominations, the endowment for this series of sermons being the gift of Dean Sage, Esq., of Brooklyn, N. Y.

Although students are not compelled to attend these services, every effort is made to attract them thither; and the result has been most gratifying. Listlessness or breaches of order in Chapel are things utterly unknown; while the attendance is large and constant. There is also in the University, a flourishing Christian Association, the members of which meet twice weekly in a room beautifully fitted up for them in the University buildings. Many of the students, however, prefer to affiliate themselves with the churches of Ithaca; and in order to permit this there is no preaching in the University Chapel on the first Sunday of the college year. Does this look like a "godless," "atheistic" or "materialistic" community?

Cornell University to-day has but three rivals in the land, and is steadily marchinng forward to a position where the arrows of its assailants cannot harm. The great trust has been managed wisely, and is fully realizing the aims and hopes of its founder and its promoters. And where is there an institution to which you can point that has accomplished so much in the same period, that has achieved a greater success in fifteen years, or with a record more proud? If any refutation of the charges, the attacks made upon it, in the past or present, were necessary, what more could be desired than this look into the history and condition of the noble institution. Truly here "a good work has been done; a good work is doing; a good work is to be done."

* * * * * * * * * *

Ezra Cornell was born at Westchester, Westchester county, N. Y., Jan. 11, 1807. His father was poor and inured to hard labor, but a man of some culture and for many winters taught district schools. He was a potter by trade and lived to the age of 91 years, having reared a family of eleven children, of whom Ezra was the eldest. The advantages Ezra enjoyed for an early education were confined to these winter schools taught by his father; nor were these always open to him except by purchase. In 1819 his father removed to DeRuyter, Madison county, N. Y., where he established a small pottery and with the assistance of Ezra and a younger brother, conducted a farm. Here his father also taught school during the winter. Ezra and his younger brother wishing to attend it, obtained their father's consent on condition that they should clear four acres of heavily timbered land by planting time in the spring. The task was accomplished by the 10th of May following. At the age of 18, without any previous apprenticeship, he cut timber and planned and built a two-story house for his father. In 1826 he began life for himself. He worked two years as a carpenter and joiner at Syracuse, Homer and other places, and in 1828, came to Ithaca, engaging with Otis Eddy to work in the machine shop attached to the cotton factory, at $3 a month and board. This sum was voluntarily increased by Mr. Eddy, at the end of six months, to $12. In 1830 he was employed by J. S. Beebe in repairing a mill. By his faithfulness and skill he won the confidence of his employer, who gave him entire charge of his milling business at a salary of $400 per annum. He continued in this position until 1840, building for his employer in the meantime a large flouring mill and engineering the construction of the since famous "tunnel," by which water is carried from the dam above the first fall in Ithaca Gorge to the mills. He also built the well-known Beebe dam at the head of the Gorge. In 1840, Mr. Beebe having failed, he purchased the right for a patent plow for the States of Maine and Georgia, and travelled through those

States selling it. While thus engaged he made the acquaintance of Francis O. J. Smith, who was interested in the then new invention, the magnetic telegraph. How by means of his inventive genius, he perfected a machine for laying wire under ground, how he improved the crude instruments of Professor Morse, making them effective on long circuits, and accomplished other achievements of immense value to telegraphy, are facts that have passed into history and need not be detailed. He received in 1844, at the hands of Hon. John C. Spencer, then Secretary of the Treasury, the position of Assistant Superintendent of the Telegraph. In May of that year he finished the line between Washington and Baltimore, and in 1845 between the latter city and New York. His salary was then $1,000 a year, of which he invested $500 in telegraph stock. In 1845 he built a line from New York to Albany, clearing thereby $6,000, and the following year organized a company and built a line from Troy to Montreal, by which he cleared $30,000. He invested much of this sum in a line from Buffalo to Milwaukee, but because of some controversy between owners of different portions of the patent, the proper fruits of this outlay were for a long time delayed. In 1855, largely through the efforts of Mr. Cornell, the rival interests were consolidated under the name of the Western Union Telegraph Company, in which he was and remained a large shareholder. He married, in 1831, Mary Ann, daughter of Benjamin Wood, of Dryden, N. Y., and his family, nearly all the time he was engaged in the telegraph business, remained in Ithaca. Great wealth flowed from his investments in the telegraph and was poured out unstintedly in behalf of many enterprises whereby his fellow-man was benefited, his beloved town enriched and his name glorified forever. Besides the Free Library and the University which he founded, his efforts in behalf of the railroad interests of the place were almost superhuman, and involved outlays of money amounting to nearly or quite $2,000,000. He never sought political distinction, but willingly served where duty called. He was in early life a Whig and in later life a Republican. He was Assemblyman in 1861-3 and State Senator from the Twenty-fourth District from 1863 to 1867. Though reared a Quaker, and holding in a measure to the views of this sect, he gave liberally in aid of other denominations. His life was beyond reproach. He was truly a great man—approachable, large-hearted, unostentatious ; the worthy poor, the struggling student, found in him a sympathizing helper ; he was equally honored by those in high and those in humble stations. His death occurred December 9, 1874, at the age of sixty-seven years. To earth was lost one of God's noblemen ; to heaven was gained a righteous spirit ; his good deeds live after him ; his name goes down to posterity with those of Peabody, Girard and Cooper.

ANDREW DICKSON WHITE, LL. D., the first and present President of Cornell University, was born at Homer, N. Y., November 7, 1832. His father was Horace White and his mother Clara Dickson White, both of New England parentage. In 1839 he went, with his father's family, to reside in Syracuse, N. Y. Having studied in the Syracuse Academy and in a private school at Ballston Spa, he entered Geneva College, now known as Hobart, in the fall of 1849, remained there one year, and then went to Yale College, where he was made an editor of the Yale Literary Magazine and took the Clark, Yale Literary and DeForest prizes, graduating in

1853. In December of the same year he went to Europe and there remained nearly three years as a student, mainly at the College of France, Paris, and the University of Berlin. He was also during seven months an attache of the American Legation at St. Petersburg. His residence covered the critical period of the Crimean War, the blockade of Cronstadt, the death of the Emperor Nicholas and the accession of Alexander II.; and of some of the more interesting events of the time he furnished accounts to sundry American journals. In 1857 he was elected Professor of History and English Literature in the University of Michigan, and interested himself greatly, in co-operation with Dr. Tappen, President at that time, and Professor Henry S. Frieze, LL. D., late acting President, in developing the institution as a University. During all this period he kept up constant business relations with Syracuse, and in 1862, on the death of his father, demands of business obliged him to give up his duties at the University of Michigan as a resident Professor, though he continued to be a non-resident Professor and Lecturer there for two years longer. His health being at the time temporarily broken, he spent a few months in Europe by the advice of his physicians, and gave his spare time there to opposing in the press, at London and Frankfort-on-the-Main, the men who were endeavoring to bring about an intervention of European powers in favor of the States in the rebellion. His main work of this kind in London (published there under the title of "A Word from the Northwest," and afterward republished in the United States) was in response to the strictures in the "American Diary" of Dr. W. H. Russell, correspondent of the London *Times*. After his return, and in the intervals of business, he found time to speak in the central part of the State on the political issues of the day, and was shortly afterward elected to the New York State Senate, and again in 1864 re-elected. While there, he gave his attention, first, to the measures necessitated by the Civil War, which was then at its height, and next to the amelioration of the condition of New York City, which at that time was prostrate under misrule. Having been appointed one of the Committee on Municipal Affairs, he devoted himself especially to a reform of the Health Department. His associates on the Committee not having been re-elected, and so having been prevented from presenting a formal report, he made, on his re-election, an informal report and speech which again brought up the subject. His earnest and judicious advocacy resulted in the reform that brought in the new Health Board, which still exists. As Chairman of the Committee on Education and Literature, he devoted himself especially to the interests of public instruction; and among other important measures, reported and advocated the bill codifying the educational laws of the State. His successful efforts to prevent the division of the land grant, which resulted in the endowment of Cornell University by Ezra Cornell and its incorporation, have been related. In 1865 he was elected to the Directorship of the School of Fine Arts founded by Mr. Street at Yale College, and to the Professorship of the History of Art at that institution. These proposals he declined. He also received the honorary degree of Doctor of Laws from the State University of Michigan at about this time. In the same year he prepared an extended report on the organization of the Cornell University, which was presented to the Trustees; and, at their first meeting, on motion of Mr. Cornell, he was unanimously elected to the Presidency of the new

THE PRESIDENT'S HOUSE.

institution. In the summer of 1866, he delivered the Phi Beta Kappa oration at Yale College, on "The Most Bitter Foe of Nations, and the Way to its Permanent Overthrow," the principal object being to show the danger of allowing a slaveholding aristocracy to survive the Civil War. In 1868 he visited Europe to examine the organization and management of the leading schools of agriculture and technology in England, France and Germany, and to purchase books and apparatus. Returning, he was present at the opening of the University for instruction and delivered an inaugural address in which he took occasion to develop more fully the plans and scope of the new institution. In this address he took ground strongly, not against classical instruction, but in favor of a greater mixture of scientific and technical education, and in favor of University methods as against the collegiate methods then mainly in use. Having been elected to the Professorship of History, he resumed his historical studies, giving instruction, mainly by lecture, in addition to his other duties. From time to time he made addresses or wrote papers presenting his ideas on education. Among these were: 1, An address upon "Scientific and Industrial Education in the United States," delivered before the New York State Agricultural Society and afterwards reprinted in the *Popular Science Monthly*. 2, A paper on the "Relation of the National and State Governments to Advanced Education,"—read before the National Educational Association at Detroit, in 1874, and afterwards reprinted in *Old and New*. 3, An address on "Education in Political Science," delivered before the Johns Hopkins University, Baltimore, at its third anniversary, in 1877. In January, 1871, he was appointed by President Grant, as one of the Government Commissioners to Santo Domingo, under the Act of Congress, the other Commissioners being Senator B. F. Wade, of Ohio, and Dr. Samuel G. Howe, of Massachusetts. In the fall of 1871 he was temporary and permanent President of the State Republican Convention at Syracuse. He was a delegate-at-large to the National Convention in 1872; was one of the electors of the State of New York at the second election of General Grant; and was also a delegate-at-large to the Republican National Convention in 1876, but was unable to attend. In 1876 he delivered before the Phi Beta Kappa Society at Brown University, and at the Cooper Institute in New York, a lecture entitled "The Battle Fields of Science." This was afterwards expanded into the treatise entitled "The Warfare of Science," published in New York in 1876, and in London, with a preface by Professor Tyndall, in the same year. He was Chairman of the Jury of Public Instruction at the Centennial Exhibition at Philadelphia in 1876. In the fall of that year he went to Europe, spending the winter at Stuttgart in historical studies, and after traveling in Germany and Italy was appointed by President Hayes an honorary Commissioner to the Paris Exposition of 1878. In this he was called, as the representative of the United States, to a place upon the Jury of Appeals, which passed upon the higher awards recommended by the lower juries. In this way he formed an extensive acquaintance among men interested in literature, science and education, not only of France, but of the various other countries of Europe. At the close of the exhibition the President of the French Republic recognized his services by conferring upon him the cross of an officer of the Legion of Honor. Returning to America in the fall of 1878, he resumed his University duties, but in the early spring of 1879 was appointed Envoy Extraordinary and Minister Plenipotentiary of the United States to the German Empire. He returned to the University in September, 1881, having found time during his stay in Germany, in addition to other duties, to study more closely than before the educational systems of Europe and to accumulate material for the University. While discharging his various political and educational trusts, Mr. White has held positions of importance in business. In the intervals of labor, and during his five visits to Europe he has collected a private library of about twenty thousand volumes, mainly in history, political and social science, and the fine arts. He has also donated to Cornell University the President's house, with its furnishings; the Horace Mann Herbarium; the White Architectural Library; a collection of architectural photographs, perhaps the richest in the world; a collection of medallions and engraved gems; a collection of photographs illustrating Civil Engineering; botanical, zoological and technical models and many works of art, which, with other contributions, make his gifts to the institution amount to considerably more than $100,000. In addition to the treatises and addresses before named Mr. White has published various articles, of which the more important are: Outlines of a Course of Lectures on History, five editions, 1860-1883; A Syllabus of a Fourth Series of Lectures on Modern History—the Greater States of Continental Europe; Review of the Governor's Message, a Speech in the New York State Senate, 1864; The Cornell University, a Speech in the New York State Senate, 1865; Address on Agricultural Education, Albany, 1869;

Report to the Trustees of Cornell University on Mr. Sage's Proposal to Endow a College for Women, 1872; Paper Money Inflation in France—How it Came, What it Brought, and How it Ended, 1876; A Bibliography of the French Revolution, published in W. O'Connor Morris's "The French Revolution and First Empire" (Epochs of History Series); Report on the Provision for Higher Instruction in Subjects bearing directly upon Public Affairs (Paris Exposition, 1878); James A. Garfield: Memorial Address, Ithaca, 1881; Cleveland Addresses (On the Education of the Freedmen and at the Dedication of Adelbert College), Ithaca, 1882; The New Germany, New York, 1882; The Message of the Nineteenth Century to the Twentieth, New Haven, 1883; Sundry articles in the *New Englander*, the *Atlantic Monthly* and the *North American Review*, 1855-81.

* * * * * * * * * *

Such is the history, such is the condition of Cornell University, and such have been the lives of the two men to whom it mainly owes its existence. The story as told is reliable, accurate. If it has not interested you continue with me no longer, for I now have only to do with facts.

EARLY HISTORY OF ITHACA.

"Since the probable visits of the Jesuit Fathers, who as early as 1657 had a mission church at Cayuga, the raiding visit of Colonel Dearborn in 1779 was the first intrusion of the white man into that part of the great wilderness which lay as a crescent at the head of Lake Tiohero (or Cayuga) and which has since become the political division known as the town of Ithaca. By this incursion of Sullivan, Cherry Valley and Wyoming had been terribly avenged, the spirit of the red warrior broken and peace brought to the land so lately the scene of war and massacre. The apprehension of any further trouble from the Indians having been allayed, it needed but the telling of the returned soldier's story embellished only with the truth concerning the physical attractions and great productiveness of the western country, to excite to enthusiasm the spirit of pioneer emigration."

In the month of April, 1788, eleven men left Kingston, on the Hudson River, with two Delaware Indians for guides, to explore the country west of the Susquehanna River, with the intention of securing a future home. They were a month or more thus employed, but returned without making a location. In April of the following year, three of their number, related to each other by marriage, Jacob Yaple, Isaac Dumond, and Peter Hinepaw, revisited the district previously explored and selected four hundred acres on lot 94, then in the county of Montgomery, of which the west line of Tioga street is now the western limit. Having planted some corn in the "Indian clearings," on the Flat, they left a younger brother of Jacob Yaple in charge of it and returned for their families. In September following they returned, bringing with them their families, a few articles of necessary household furniture, some farming utensils and a few hogs, sheep, cattle and horses.

The three families numbered twenty persons—Jacob Yaple, his wife and three children; John Yaple, the brother; Isaac Dumond, his wife and three children; John Dumond and his wife; and Peter Hinepaw and his wife and three children. A month was consumed in their journey to Owego, where there was a small settlement, and nineteen days thence to Ithaca. Between Owego and the head of Cayuga Lake was only a well-beaten Indian trail, along which the way had to be cleared through the forest. Arrived at their new home three log cabins were soon erected, the first on the north side of Cascadilla Creek, where Williams' Mill now stands, which was occupied by the Hinepaw family, and the other two, occupied by the Yaple and Dumond families, on the spot now covered by the residence of Adam S. Cowdry, on East State Street. The Indians proved friendly and gave the new-comers substantial assistance. In summer they occupied the higher ground with their wigwams, but at the approach of winter "pitched their tents" in the gorge of Six Mile Creek. The second year after the coming of the white people, however, the greater portion of the Indians removed to their reservation at the north end of the lake.

Game was abundant in the adjacent forests, affording the table rare bits of deer and bear, while the lake and its tributaries sheltered and supported the choicest of the finny tribes. Long journeys were required at first to supply the families with flour, but in the second year of the settlement Jacob Yaple built a small mill on the Cascadilla, near Mr. Hinepaw's cabin, which was capable of grinding 20 or 25 bushels of grain per day. Other families soon followed these pioneers, but in the years 1791-93 when the roads or great "turnpikes," mainly following an easterly and westerly direction, were being pushed forward into the wilderness, giving to the pioneers means of more frequent communication with their friends and kin in the older settlements, the families of the Yaples, Dumonds and Hinepaw had the misfortune to lose their lands by reason of the carelessness or wickedness of their agent, who was to attend to the payment of installments and taxes in Albany, and it passed out of their possession.

Simeon DeWitt then came into possession of nearly all the domain, which is now embraced within the bounds of the village corporation, as well as other lands outside that limit, and laid out the plot of a village to which he gave the name of Ithaca. He encouraged settlement by the liberal terms offered in the sale of his lands, but for about ten years after its first settlement the little hamlet on the flats increased very little in population, there being not more than half a dozen houses in 1798. The country about was filling up more rapidly and patches of clearing here and there foretold the doom of the late unbroken wilderness. The natural advantages of Ithaca were soon widely known, however, and enterprising men came in to make use of her lake and streams for commercial and manufacturing purposes, and the succeeding decade was a period of accelerated growth, the hamlet becoming a village.

In a letter dated Ithaca, May 8, 1810, Mr. DeWitt wrote: "I find this village considerably increased since I was here before. I have counted thirty-eight dwelling houses, among which are one very large, elegant three-story house for a hotel, and five of two stories; the rest of one story—all generally neat frame buildings. Besides these there is a school house and buildings for merchant's stores, and shops for carpenters, cabinet-makers, blacksmiths, coopers, tanners; and we have besides shoemakers, tailors, two lawyers, one doctor, watch cleaner, turner, miller, hatters, etc., etc." The south side of the

Cascadilla, in the vicinity of the cabin of Mr. Hinepaw and the mill of Mr. Yaple, became a sort of centre of trade and manufacture at the earliest period of Ithaca's history, but fifteen or twenty years later Aurora street, between Six Mile Creek and the Cascadilla, in turn became the business centre, and here were located the taverns, stores, factories, tanneries, etc.

The public road built from Oxford, on the Chenango River, directly through to Ithaca, in 1791-93 became the great highway for immigration in the southern part of the State for many years, and in 1804 the Susquehanna and Bath Turnpike was incorporated, running through the present towns of Caroline, Dryden, Ithaca and Enfield, what is now State street (earlier Owego) forming a part of the road. The Owego and Ithaca Turnpike Company, incorporated in 1807, was finished in 1811, as was also the road to Geneva, by the Geneva and Ithaca Turnpike Company. These roads gave to the little village of Ithaca considerable importance; the business of the place was stimulated by the demand for Cayuga plaster, which sprung up during the last war with England, when the supply from Nova Scotia was cut off. Immense quantities were transported from Ithaca by team to Owego, from whence by the river the lower markets were supplied.

Governor Clinton evidently believed it to be a place of growing importance as early as 1810, for he thus wrote in his journal: "The situation of this place, at the head of Cayuga Lake, and a short distance from the descending waters to the Atlantic, and about 120 miles to the descending waters to the Mississippi, must render it a place of great importance." It was certainly starting well and steadily increased in size and importance, and when the act of Legislature creating Tompkins County was passed April 17, 1817, Ithaca was designated as the county seat. This act contained a provision that in case of failure to convey a site for the county buildings to the supervisors, and the securing of $7,000 to be paid, the new county was to be re-annexed to the counties of Cayuga and Seneca from whence it was taken. The citizens of Tompkins manifested a lively interest in the matter, the provisions in the enactment were complied with and in 1818 a wooden structure was erected and ready for occupancy as a court house and jail on the site occupied by the present court house on East Mill street.

In 1820 Ithaca contained a population of 859 persons, and on the second day of April, 1821, was incorporated as a village—just seventeen days after the town of Ithaca was formed from Ulysses. Of these 859 people, 5 were foreigners, not naturalized; 10 were engaged in agriculture; 10 in commerce, and 143 in manufactures, including mechanics of every description. The formation of a new town to be called by its name was in appreciation of the growth and promising future of the village, which was just at this time being favored with an important addition to its transportation facilities—a steamboat "to ply from one end to the other of Cayuga Lake." The Cayuga Steamboat Company had been organized in 1819, and on March 18, 1820, the keel of the "Enterprise" was laid, and on the 4th of May following the finished vessel was launched midst the huzzas of the people and the firing of cannon. She was 80 by 30 feet over all and of 120 tons burden, with an engine of 24 horse-power, her machinery being made in Jersey City and brought to Ithaca by teams. The *Journal* of June 7, 1820, made the follwing announcement: "The Enterprise is connected with the line of stages from Newburgh to Buffalo, and thus furnishes to travellers from New York, and others going west, one of the most expeditious and pleasant routes in the State. The stage runs from Newburgh to this village in *two days*. Thus travellers may leave New York at 5 o'clock P. M. in the steamboat; the second day arrive at Ithaca; go on board the steamboat 'Enterprise' the same night; receive good accommodations and rest in comfortable *births* during the passage; resume the stage next morning at Cayuga bridge, and the same night arrive at Buffalo; *making the whole route in three days!*—one day sooner than it is performed by way of Albany."

Although these transportation facilities are now considered insignificant, they then attracted considerable attention and trade to Ithaca, and the possibilities thus presented of more rapid advancement with greater facilities doubtless promoted the project of a railway to Owego. The Ithaca and Owego railroad was incorporated January 28, 1828, and it was opened in April, 1834. The road was 29 miles long and had two "inclined planes" ascending from Ithaca, the first, 1733 feet long, with a rise of one foot in 4 28-100 feet, making a total rise of 405 feet, and the second or upper, 2225 feet long, with a rise of one foot in every twenty-one feet. "The old style flat or strap rail was used throughout and for six years horse power was employed exclusively, the steeper plane being overcome by stationary power in the form of a huge windlass housed at the summit and worked also by horses—generally blind."*

In the meantime other steamboats had made their appearance upon the lake and great progress was making by the village—but the following bit of contemporaneous history, condensed from Solomon Southwick's statements respecting the trades, manufactures, &c., of Ithaca, as he found them in 1834, will give the best idea of its progress: "Newspapers—*The Journal*, by Nathan Randall; *Chronicle*, by D. D. and A. Spencer; *Jeffersonian* and *Tompkins Times*, by Charles Robbins. Bookstores, 2; dry goods merchants, 23; hardware 2;"jewelers, 3; druggists, 3; grocers, 16; millinery establishments, 5. Of mechanical establishments, embracing all classes, there were 36, in which were employed 289 people." The principal manufacturers apart from the "mechanical establishments" just named, were "Mack, Andrus & Woodruff's paper mill employing 30 hands—this firm's printing office, book bindery and book store employ 23 hands; J. S. Beebe's *Olympic Falls* Flouring Mill, conducted by Ezra Cornell; J. S. Beebe's Plaster Mill—turned out 800 tons of plaster last year; Lucas Levinsworth's Machine Shop, employing 12 hands—manufactures pails, tubs, keelers, &c.; Barnaby & Hedges' Chair Factory in the machine shop building—makes 200 chairs yearly; Dennis & Vail's Ithaca Furnace—an extensive establishment—makes mill gearing and other castings and has been in operation six years; there is another furnace near this, owned by H. King, which melts 75 tons of iron yearly; Silas Mead's plow manufactory—makes about 200 plows yearly; S. J. Blythe's Woolen Factory—this factory dresses from 500 to 700 pieces of cloth and cards about 14,000 pounds of wool annually; John Raymond's Wool-

* The road was sold at auction by the Comptroller, May 20, 1842; bought by the "Cayuga and Susquehanna Railroad Co." and sold by them in 1849 to New York parties who rebuilt it, laying heavy iron as far as the "upper switch" station in December of that year and in the spring following extending the road to the pier at the head of the lake, descending the hill by a circuitous route, as now. In 1855 it was leased to the D., L. & W R. R. Co., who have since operated it.

en Factory—does business in **kind and amount similar to Mr. Blythe's**; Cook & Conrad's Ithaca Iron Foundry and Steam Engine Works—business nearly the same as that of Dennis & Vail, and turns out a large amount of work; Factory of Hardy & Rich, manufacturers of saw mill dogs—this dog is a patented article and sells at $150 a set—total business $7,500 annually—lumber sawed with this dog brought **50 cents** extra per 1000 feet."

From this statement it will be inferred that **Ithaca was an** embryo city from which much was hoped. Indeed, it gave **indications of such a** rapid growth that "the year 1836 **was a period** of wild speculation. **Land increased fabulously in** price; whole farms were laid out in city lots and scarce an acre within two miles of the village was purchasable for tillage. Banking institutions, railroads and canals multiplied in brains and upon charts with astonishing facility. Several of **the** first were formally organized, but never proceeded **to business.** The *Journal* of July in that year reports that a sale of sundry water-powers at Fall Creek brought at auction $220,000; and further says, 'a parcel of the DeWitt estate, which was purchased last December for $4,676, sold at auction on the 6th for $52,929. A farm adjoining the village, which was purchased last summer for $50 per acre, has recently been sold for $500 per acre, and the purchaser has been offered and declined an advance on his purchase.' There was but one ending possible **to** this—the foamy period of Ithaca's history. A short time served to blow the froth from **many a** supposed full glass, and reveal the very small *bier* at the bottom."

But it was not without some reason that these bright anticipations and the consequent speculation was indulged in. With its railroad and steamboat lines Ithaca became the central shipping point for all this region, business of all kinds flourished and enterprising men were investing their money freely in every enterprise that promised success. The tide was taken **at its flood, but did** not lead on to the great sisterhood of cities, however, and Ithaca settled down to a steady, healthful growth.

In 1858 the population of the *town* of Ithaca was 7,153, which had only increased in 1866 to 7,264. Recovering from the effects of the "foamy period", the village became somewhat conservative and grew slowly, but its growth was marked by a substantiality that was more desirable. The opening of the Ithaca and Athens Railroad* and the Ithaca and Cortland Railroad† in 1871, the Geneva and Ithaca Railroad in 1873 and the Cayuga Lake Railroad‡ in 1874, affording the most desirable transportation facilities, gave it another slight impetus and it again began to move forward, as is shown by a population in 1880 of 11,896 in the town.

From a village with the appearance of having a "mushroom" growth it became characterized by its appearance of solidity and wealth; handsome residences, substantial business blocks and fine streets were its features, and Ithaca assumed

---

* The Ithaca and Athens Railroad and the Geneva and Ithaca Railroad were consolidated in 1874 and were purchased by the Lehigh Valley R. R. Co., and are now known as the Geneva, Ithaca & Sayre Railroad.

† The Ithaca and Cortland Railroad was consolidated in 1871 with the Utica, Horseheads & Elmira Railroad and became the Utica, Ithaca & Elmira Railroad.

‡ The Cayuga Lake Railroad runs along the east side of the Lake; it was purchased in 1876 by the Lehigh Valley Railroad Company.

the garb of a typical and, it might be said, a model University town. During the past few years an era of prosperity seems to have set in, its older manufactories have received new life, new ones have been established, every branch of business became more prosperous—Ithaca to-day is in the most thriving condition, and its future is probably brighter than at any period during its history.

ITS CHURCHES.

There are fifteen churches in Ithaca, in which worship eight religious denominations—Presbyterian, Baptist, Roman Catholic, Congregational, Episcopal, Methodist, Free Methodist and Unitarian. The Presbyterian Church was organized in 1804, the first church was built in 1818, and the present edifice in DeWitt Park in 1853. The first Methodist services were held in 1793, the first church built in 1820 and the edifice now occupied at the corner of Aurora and Mill streets in 1866. The second Methodist church was organized in 1851 from the parent society and in the same year a wooden structure was built on the corner of Seneca and Plain streets; the edifice now occupied at the corner of State and Albany streets was erected in 1878. St. John's Episcopal Church was organized in 1822, the first church built in 1824, and the edifice now occupied at the corner of Seneca and Cayuga streets erected in 1860. St. Paul's Episcopal Church was organized in 1874; services are held in the University Chapel. Episcopal services are also held in Christ Chapel, on Cliff street. The first Baptist society, (Park Baptist Church) was organized in 1826, the first church built in 1831 and the edifice now occupied on the east side of DeWitt Park erected in 1854. The Tabernacle Baptist Church was organized in 1870; they have a small house of worship on Railroad avenue, near Tioga street. The first Congregational Church was organized as a Dutch Reformed Church in 1830 and an edifice erected in 1830-31; in 1872 the church became a congregational society and a handsome new church is now building on the old site at the corner of Seneca and Geneva streets. The Church of the Immaculate Conception (Roman Catholic) was organized in 1834, the first church was built in 1851 with the title of St. Luke's, and the edifice now occupied at the corner of Seneca and Geneva streets, erected in 1860; this parish is now building a parochial school building on West Buffalo street, at a cost of $12,000, to be taught by the "Sisters of St. Joseph." The African M. E. Zion Church was organized in 1833 and subsequently built a modest church on Wheat street which they still occupy. The Wesleyan (colored) M. E. Church is an offshoot from the preceding and was organized in 1851; their Church stands on North Albany street. The first Unitarian Society was organized in 1865 and their church on the north side of Buffalo street, near Aurora, was erected in 1873. The Free Methodist Society was organized in 1871; their church stands on North Tioga street, near Farm. The Union Church of Fall Creek was organized in 1877 and has a small edifice on North Aurora, near Tompkins street.

PUBLIC SCHOOLS.

In educational facilities Ithaca presents advantages that are equalled by few localities in this country, the courses of study being complete, in continuity and thoroughness, from the time of entering the primaries until graduation at Cornell University.

As early as 1796 that portion of the town of Ulysses which became Ithaca was represented in the management of the existing schools by Robert McDowell, Benjamin Pelton and William VanOrman—early settlers—as is shown by the town records, but when or where the first school house was erected is not known. In 1825 an academy was opened in the present high school building which was conducted with more or less success until 1875, but the only free schools in the village during this period, after the abandonment of the old Lancasterian school at Geneva and Mill streets in 1854, were one large school (now the Central School) in which all grades were taught, and a branch primary school. In 1874 an act of Legislature authorized the establishment of a Union School District with a complete graded school system under the control of a Board of Education consisting of twelve members. Under authority of this act a new school building was erected on West Hill and two temporary schools opened on East and South Hills in 1874, and in September, 1875, a high school was organized in the old academy building, which had been transferred to the Board of Education for that purpose. And from this beginning the movement continued onward and upward until Ithaca's public school system was regarded as being without a superior in the State. In 1879 a large new building was erected at Fall Creek ; in 1880 the Central School building was remodelled, in 1881 a new building was erected on East Hill and now a new high school building is to be erected during the coming year, on the old site, at a cost of $50,000. There are now six school buildings, in which are employed 34 teachers, and the whole number of pupils registered in all the schools during 1882-3 was 2,020, an increase of 74 over the preceding year. The rank of the High School in the apportionment of the Literature Fund in 1882 was thirteenth, which means that but 12 schools in the State received more from that fund on account of instruction of academic pupils, while there were 210 that received less. The courses of study in the schools, as previously stated, is most complete, from the entrance into the primaries until graduation from the High School, when students are prepared to enter the University.

ITS NEWSPAPERS.

Journalism in Ithaca is far in advance of "village" journalism in general, and in the *Journal, Democrat* and *Ithacan* the "Forest City" possesses able champions of its interests and highly creditable representatives of the modern "press". The *Ithaca Journal* was established nearly two years before the county of Tompkins was formed, and has not only kept pace with its progress, but, if anything, in advance of it, and is now a more representative newspaper than many of great pretensions issuing from the larger cities. Its first issue was made on Independence Day, 1815, as the *Seneca Republican*, a weekly newspaper, by Jonathan Ingersoll. Early in the year following its name was changed to the *American Journal*, and was purchased by Ebenezer Mack and Searing, who early in 1823 changed the title to *Ithaca Journal*. From this time until December, 1833, it was published by Mr. Mack and his different business partners. In 1827 the title was the *Ithaca Journal, Literary Gazette and General Advertiser*; about one year later a portion of

this name was dropped, and it became the *Ithaca Journal and Advocate*. In 1833 it was sold to Nathan Randall; in 1837, Randall sold to Mattison & Barnaby, and in 1839 A. E. Barnaby sold to Alfred Wells, who soon after sold to J. H. Selkreg, who from that time until February, 1877, continued its publication. The *Journal* has merged into itself many rival publications—the *Jeffersonian and Tompkins Times*, in 1837; the *Flag of Our Union*, in 1849, and in 1870 the *Ithacan* being included in the number. After many unavailing efforts to start a daily paper in Ithaca and make it live, the *Daily Journal* made its debut on the first day of July, 1872. It risked the large membership fee and the heavy weekly dues necessary to secure connection with the Associated Press; large investments in fast running presses, type and other material and paraphernalia; and the salaries of an increased force of writers and compositors required by such an undertaking. The previous several attempts had whetted the public appetite and prepared the way for this effort, and although not a profitable venture in its earlier years, owing to the considerable expenditures necessarily incurred in its establishment, it has gradually but constantly gained in public appreciation and patronage, until it has already become more than self sustaining; one of the most important institutions of the county, with a prospect of great prosperity and usefulness. In February, 1877, the business of the daily and weekly *Journals*, with the large job printing and other incidental departments, had attained such proportions that an increase of capital and division of labor became imperative. A stock company was accordingly formed under the general laws of the State and incorporated as the "Ithaca Journal Association." Of this organization John H. Selkreg is President; Charles M. Benjamin, Vice President; and George E. Priest, Secretary and Treasurer. The contrast between the hand press on which the earlier *Journal* was laboriously worked and the rapid steam cylinder presses it now employs affords no greater idea of the march of improvement than the primitive third floor office—sanctum, composing and press room, all in one—of 1815 compared with the stately *Journal* block erected in 1872, with its elegant appointments and every convenience. In its long career the *Journal* has never been neutral in politics, but for the greater time strongly partisan. Originally Democratic, it continued so until 1856, when the slavery question becoming the paramount issue, it became Republican, and has ever since espoused the best interests of that party, wielding no small influence in the county and State.

The *Ithaca Democrat* was established in 1820 by D. D. Spencer under the title of the *Ithaca Chronicle*. In 1828 Anson Spencer became associated with him in its publication, and it was continued by them until 1833, when Anson Spencer became sole proprietor and published it until 1855, when it passed into the hands of A. E. Barnaby & Co., who issued it as the *American Citizen*. It subsequently came into the possession of Anson Spencer, who published it until 1863, when it was consolidated with the *Tompkins County Democrat*. This paper dated its existence from 1856, when it was started by Timothy Maloney and continued by him until his death in 1860. In 1861 S. C. Clisbe became its owner, but soon after sold a half interest to B. R. Williams, and these gentlemen issued it until its consolidation with the *American Citizen*. The consolidated papers were issued by Spencer & Williams as the *Ithaca Citizen and Democrat* until July 4th, 1867, when it was enlarged and the name changed to the *Ithaca Democrat*. Mr. Spencer succeeded to the sole ownership and remained its editor and proprietor until December 1st, 1873, when Ward Gregory became associated with him in its publication and assumed editorial charge in 1874. Upon the death of Mr. Spencer in 1876 Mr. Gregory became sole owner of the *Democrat*. He thoroughly renovated the printing establishment and by energy and perseverance, placed the office upon a paying basis. It is the only Democratic paper in Tompkins county and justly merits its success.

The *Weekly Ithacan* was established at Dryden, in May, 1856, by H. D. Rumsey, under the name of *Rumsey's Companion*. It was soon after changed to the *Fireside Companion*, and again in a month, to the *Dryden News*. In 1857 it was purchased by G. B. House, and the title changed to the *New York Confederacy*, and soon after discontinued. In July, 1858, Ashael Clapp resuscitated the paper as the *Dryden Weekly News*, which he continued to publish at Dryden, several times enlarging and otherwise improving it, until April, 1871, when in company with Messrs. Norton and Cunningham, the paper with the half of its entire subscription list, was removed to Ithaca, and here issued as the *Weekly Ithacan and Dryden News*. In six months this partnership was dissolved, Mr. Clapp resuming the entire control. In June, 1874, the paper was sold to George Ketchum, but he failed to make a success of its management and the office was closed by the Sheriff. After some delay, the right of ownership reverted to Mr. Clapp, who held a mortgage on the paper, and by dint of enterprise and industry he restored the paper to its former standing, and largely increased its circulation. The *Ithacan* is a large eight-page paper, and its prosperous condition is very gratifying to Mr. Clapp, and the friends of the causes which he advocates—temperance and "greenbackism."

PUBLIC BUILDINGS AND GROUNDS.

The Cornell Free Library occupies a fine three-story brick building on the corner of Seneca and Tioga streets, and contains over 11,000 volumes which, with a few necessary exceptions, circulate free within the limits of Tompkins County. The institution owes its existence to the public spirit and munificence of the late Hon. Ezra Cornell, and very appropriately bears his name. The Cornell Library Association was incorporated April 5, 1864, and under this act Mr. Cornell caused to be erected the building which was dedicated with appropriate ceremonies on the evening of December 20, 1866, and with the ground upon which it stands presented to the village. It is 68x104 feet in dimensions and cost $75,000. Besides the library and reading room, the building contains a fine hall for public exercises and other excellent rooms for business purposes, whose rental was designed to sustain the library free of cost to patrons. It has more than accomplished this purpose, the receipts proving sufficient to pay expenses and add yearly many volumes to the library.

The other public buildings worthy of note are the court-house and jail, on East Mill street, erected respectively in the years 1855 and 1850; Wilgus Opera House, corner of State and Tioga streets, erected in 1869 by H. L. Wilgus at a cost of $60,000, and the Post-Office, on East State above Cayuga street.

The cemetery, covering 16 acres of the hill slope on the north side of the Cascadilla, with its natural advantages in the variety of its surface, its native growth of trees and commanding views, is an oject of admiration to visitors.

There are several very pretty little parks scattered throughout the village, chief among which are DeWitt and Washington Parks, both near the centre of the town. The large grounds of the Tompkins County Agricultural Society, on which successful fairs and cattle shows are annually held, are situated in the southern extremity of the village.

LOCAL GOVERNMENT.

The village is divided into four wards, and is governed by a President and Board of Trustees, composed of two members from each ward. An efficient force of four sturdy policemen, under command of a chief, are the guardians of the peace.

Property is amply protected against fire by an excellent fire department, composed of eight companies—three steamers, three hose companies, one hook and ladder company and an organization known as protective police, (composed principally of the best known business men) whose duty it is to take charge of and protect property removed from burning buildings.

WATER AND GAS.

An abundant supply of water is furnished by the Ithaca Water Works, a private corporation. The water is drawn from Buttermilk Creek at a point two miles south, the stream being 215 feet above the business portion of the village. Three reservoirs of immense capacity are employed, one being located at the point on the stream mentioned, a second, for storage purposes, a half mile above, and the third on South Hill, which in connection with the first named is used for distributing purposes. From these two reservoirs the water enters iron mains and under a pressure of 90 pounds to the square inch is carried to all parts of the village. For fire purposes hydrants are located at convenient points, from which strong streams can be thrown over the highest building.

Gas is supplied by the same corporation

ITS FACILITIES AND RESOURCES.

Exceptional facilties are possessed by Ithaca for the successful conduct of almost every branch of manufacturing or mercantile business. Four railways and a steamboat line afford the most desirable transportation facilities : The southern outlets are the Delaware Lackawanna and Western Railroad Company, operating the railway between Ithaca and Owego, where connections are made with the main line of this company and the Erie Railroad both East and West, and the Geneva, Ithaca and Sayre Railroad, operated by the Lehigh Valley Railroad Company, and connecting at Sayre with the main line of the Lehigh Valley Railroad, the competition between these lines to and from New York being highly beneficial. An outlet north is had by the Geneva, Ithaca and Sayre Railroad connecting at Geneva with the Auburn branch of the New York Central Railroad, and at Lyons with the main line of the New York Central; by the Cayuga Lake Railroad, connecting at Cayuga, with the Auburn branch of the same road, and the Cayuga Lake Steamboat Line, with the same last named connections, while all these lines have a lively competitor in the Utica, Ithaca and Elmira Railroad, which connects at Elmira with the Erie, and at Canastota with the West Shore and New York Central Railroads. The Erie Canal is also made accessible by Cayuga Lake, being intersected at Cayuga, and a considerable portion of the heavier freights—grain and coal—is carried over the Lake to this canal. Three banks—the First National, Tompkins County National and the Ithaca Savings Bank—afford unexceptionable banking facilities and the telegraph, telephone,* mail and express service is most complete. Its hotels are really excellent—in fact, Ithaca possesses nearly all the advantages of a city without many of the disadvantages incident thereto, and may fairly be characterized as an equally desirable location for business or pleasure. But that it is not simply a "University town" or dependent solely upon its attractiveness of location and scenery for notice will be admitted by the visitor if the trouble is taken to inspect the piano and organ, the calendar clock, the autophone and the glass factories, the gun works, the agricultural implement manufactories and other industrial establishments that are giving it a name and a place among the manufacturing towns of Central New York, whose products are attaining a national reputation. And for the benefit of those that cannot, brief historical and descriptive sketches of its resourses—of the leading manufacturing and mercantile establishments— will be presented, with the belief that to many they will prove interesting, and to those for whom they have no interest, I can only say: "Beg pardon for their introduction, but to the village of Ithaca these establishments are of more vital import than all its magnificent scenery, and therefore must have equal representation."

THE FOREST CITY MIXED PAINT WORKS.

Of all the manufacturing interests in Ithaca, none are more fully entitled to recognition in this work than the Forest City Mixed Paint Works. Although established but a couple of years, and giving employment to fewer workmen, probably, than some of the other industries, the benefits the village must eventually derive from this industry, the superior character of the products of which will undoubtedly cause it to grow and become one of the large labor-employing concerns, are such that it is not only worthy a prominent position in ITHACA AND ITS RESOURCES, but deserving the fullest support and encouragement of residents of the "Forest City." And it is seldom, too, in these days, when the cities and towns of the East and West are vieing with each other in their efforts to secure the location of manufacturing enterprises in their midst, that a manufacturer with both capital and ability settles in a locality without receiving some valuable consideration as an inducement, without any other expectation than that solely by the merit of his products is he to benefit by adding his quota to the resources, the wealth, prosperity and industrial reputation of a place.

That a prejudice against ready-mixed paint exists—fostered principally by painters for obvious reasons—there is no denying, but this prejudice is rapidly being overcome, just as has been overcome the prejudices that from time immemorial have obstructed the progress of labor-saving inventions and other innovations that have proven a boon to mankind. True, it is sometimes not without

---

* See sketch entitled "Ithaca Telephone Service."

reason this prejudice exists, for in this as in all other branches of business there are persons who care not for reputation and produce and sell great quantities of an article at an immense profit until the people discover its worthlessness, when they abandon its manufacture and engage in some other scheme for deluding the public. But when a responsible manufacturer places an article upon the market which he guarantees to be as represented, prejudices so formed should not be allowed to prevent its trial, especially when there is every reason to believe such trial will prove beneficial.

And it is now generally admitted that ready-mixed paints, when produced by responsible manufacturers, are far superior and more preferable to paints mixed in the old way just as required. This favorable feeling is doubtless largely owing to the fact that people are becoming more generally acquainted with the process of manufacturing these paints, and when this process is fully understood they readily perceive why ready-mixed paints can be sold cheaper than they can buy the material and mix it themselves, and are in other respects more preferable.

The Forest City Mixed Paint Works, at the corner of State and Meadow streets, possess facilities for the production of these paints that are unsurpassed by any manufacturer in the country. The building occupied is a three-story frame structure, 66 x 75 feet in dimensions, and is thoroughly equipped with the most improved machinery and conveniently arranged according to the advanced ideas of the proprietor, Mr. J. W. Tibbetts, the motive power for driving the machinery being furnished by an engine of ten-horse power. The material is carried on elevators and the oil pumped to the third story, where the lumps are crushed and the proper quantities of oil and other material weighed out and by an ingenious arrangement conducted to the mixing tanks on the second floor. Rapidly turning agitators in these tanks thoroughly mix the material until it has assumed the character of ordinary paint, when it is permitted to run into the mills for grinding. One of these mills is connected with each tank and the grinding is conducted in the most systematic and economical manner, as, indeed, is the whole process. When ground the paint is ready for use, possessing the proper consistency and being entirely devoid of sediment, and is sent down to the first floor, where it is put up in packages for sale and shipment. Thus it will be seen that large quantities of paint can be thoroughly mixed and ground at a slight cost, comparatively, while the advantages of having the material mixed and ground under the superintendence of a specialist are obvious. Forest City Mixed Paints are manufactured under Mr. Tibbetts' personal supervision from pure white lead and oxide of zinc, ground in pure linseed oil. The raw material is first quality, purchased direct from the mines, and the oil is the purest linseed that is boiled. And as an earnest of his assertions as to the purity of his mixed paints, Mr. Tibbett's has frequently been heard to offer a forfeit of a thousand dollars for any adulteration discovered in the material used in the manufacture of Forest City Mixed Paints.

Thirty-two distinct colors are manufactured at the Forest City Mixed Paint Works, and as an illustration of the popularity and reputation they are acquiring it might be mentioned that C. E. Clark, architect of the National Capitol, at Washington, D. C., gives these paints the preference over those of all other manufacturers. Forest City Mixed Paint is not only unchangeable in color, economical and durable, but is superior on account of its body and wearing properties, and as this fact becomes more fully known the demand for it must still more largely increase and this industry become of still more value to the business interests of Ithaca.

Mr. Tibbetts' spent his boyhood's days in Ithaca, and when the war of the rebellion burst upon the country, went out as a volunteer with Colonel Baker's First California Regiment, and just in time, too, to take part in the first battle of Bull Run. At the end of his two year's service, he again enlisted, this time with the 109th New York Regiment, and thus spent four years in the service of his country, being promoted from the ranks to the captaincy of a company. Coming home at the close of the war, and feeling the need of a business education, he entered a Commercial College at Poughkeepsie, and after a course of study there engaged in the mercantile business at Pond Eddy, N. Y. Here he remained about eight years, meeting with success in his business ventures and marrying an estimable lady. Having become prosperous, and the father of a couple bright children, a few years ago he disposed of his business in Pond Eddy, and removed to his old home in Ithaca to give his children the advantages of the society and education it so fully confers. He then purchased an interest in the Superior Paint Company of Havana, N. Y., and becoming familiar with the manufacture of mixed paints and discovering that he possessed a special aptitude for the business, after a couple years bought out his partners and removed the business in 1880 to Ithaca, believing that by the production of a superior article it could be developed into a large industry. Purchasing the property at the corner of State and Meadow streets, he razed to the ground the old building formerly standing there, and erected the fine factory he now occupies. The business has about doubled with each succeeding year, but he has expended a large amount of money in bringing the merits of Forest City Mixed Paint to the notice of the public, and it has not as yet had time to fully return. But it will, and the prediction is ventured that the decided merit and superiority of his paint will in a short time make the Forest City Paint Works one of the largest industries of the kind in the country. Mr. Tibbetts, is a liberal and enterprising as well as far seeing and shrewd business man and deserving the great success in this business which must eventually be his, and which should be the reward of every man who resolutely determines to produce the best article of the kind manufactured or nothing.

THE ITHACA CALENDAR CLOCK COMPANY.

An industry that has done much to make the name of Ithaca known throughout the world is the manufacture of calendar clocks, an article now acknowledged to be indispensable to every place of business—a necessity in every office, in every household. And it is with justifiable pride that this industry can be spoken of, for not only is here produced the only perfectly reliable calendar clock manufactured, but these clocks have made their way into all parts of the world, spreading the name and the fame of the "Forest City" in nearly every habitable part of the globe. Much skill and ingenuity have been expended in bringing to a state of perfection the mechanism producing such wonderful results, and the Ithaca Calendar Clock, indicating perpetually the day of the month, the month of the year, the hour of the day and the day of the week, is really one of the wonders of the progress and development of the Nineteenth Century. It is accomplished by a perpetual mechanical calendar of the most ingenious construction, connected with superior eight and thirty day (either weight or spring) clock movements. The calendars are printed in the English, Spanish, Portugese, French, German, Russian, Turkish and Asiatic languages, and the clocks are manufactured in numerous styles, ranging widely in prices to suit the various wants of the public. They are the only calendar clocks that received a certificate of award at the International Exhibition at Philadelphia in 1876, at Sydney in 1879, and at Melbourne in 1880.

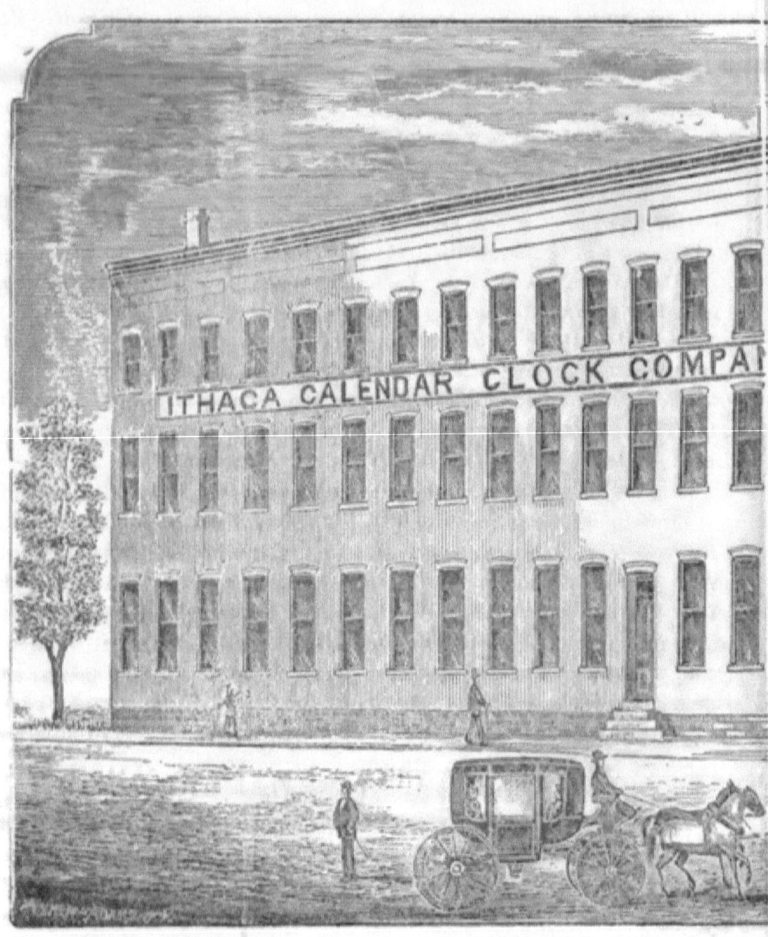

The first calendar carried by clock machinery in America was invented by J. H. Hawes, of Ithaca, and was patented in 1853. This calendar was imperfect, as it would not make the change of the 29th of February, in leap year. In 1854 W. H. Akins invented an improvement on this calendar, automatic in its operations, readjusting itself to show all the changes, including the 29th of February. This calendar was purchased by

Huntington & Platts and placed by them in the hands of the Mix Brothers, of Ithaca, for manufacture. Still further improvements were made by the Mix Brothers, for which patents were granted in 1860 and 1862, and the Messrs. Huntington & Platts continued to manufacture large bank calendar clocks for a year or two, and then disposed of their patents to the Seth Thomas Clock Company of Connecticut. During 1864-5 Mr. Horton, of Ithaca, invented a new and almost perfect perpetual calendar, and in April, 1865, obtained his first patent, in eight distinct claims. This calendar, subsequently improved and made absolutely perfect, is the one owned and used only by the Ithaca Calendar Clock Company,

and which has given them virtually a monopoly of the calendar clock business of the world.

Horton interested several gentlemen in his invention and in August, of 1868, the Ithaca Calendar Clock Company was formed for the purpose of producing calendar clocks under his patents, the officers of the company being John H. Selkreg, President; Samuel P. Sherwood, Vice President, and William J. Storms,

Secretary and Treasurer. The capital of the company was only $800, and operations were begun on a very modest scale in a single room located directly opposite Treman Bros. shop on Cayuga street. The clocks possessing both merit and novelty met with a large sale and in a short time this single room had become entirely inadequate for the business. About 1869 J. B. Williams fitted up his three story brick building on State street for the company, into which they removed and continued the manufacture of the calendar clocks on a much larger scale, the capacity after the removal being about twenty times greater. Here they remained until 1874, when Messrs. Selkreg and Sherwood were succeeded by Messrs. B. G. Jayne and Hervey Platts as President and Vice President, respectively, the capital of the company was increased to $150,000, and large three story brick buildings were erected on the old Tompkins County Fair Grounds, at Adams, Auburn, Dey and Franklin streets. These buildings formed a hollow square, 100x130 feet in dimensions and here again the capacity was largely increased. An immense number of calendar clocks were annually produced and placed upon the market, and it was apparently thought the production could not be too great. In February, 1876, the works were destroyed by fire. They were immediately rebuilt, however, but in the fall of 1877 Charles H. White succeeded Mr. Storms as Secretary and Treasurer, and H. M. Durphy was given the superintendence and general management of the concern and the more conservative and wise conduct of its affairs that has since characterized its management has proven decidedly profitable. At the election of officers in January, 1883, Messrs. F. C. Cornell, Francis M Finch and Charles H. White were respectively chosen to fill the offices of President, Vice President and Secretary and Treasurer, and the Ithaca Calendar Clock Company is probably now in the most highly prosperous condition it has ever been About 6,000 calendar clocks are annually produced, which, selling at prices ranging from $10 to $75 each, bring into Ithaca a large aggregate amount of money, and as a force of about 34 people are employed, chiefly the more skilled mechanics, the industry is of great value to the place.

The works of this company occupying the square bounded by Adams, Auburn, Dey and Franklin streets, present to the visitor an interesting exhibit of some of the most ingenious special machinery ever invented. As previously stated, the buildings are three story brick structures arranged in the form of a hollow square, part of them, however, being now occupied by the Autophone Company. A 75-horse power boiler furnishes steam for heating purposes, as also supplying the 50-horse power engine driving the machinery, and the entire plant, in its completeness and convenience, is a characteristic sample of American enterprise. One of the interesting features is an electric arrangement for detecting any failure on the part of the watchman to discharge faithfully his duties, and another, the machine invented for the purpose of testing the workings of the calendars, and by which they are run through all the changes of eight years of time before leaving the factory, none being shipped until they have passed this test and been proven in all respects accurate and reliable. All of the machinery, however, is specially adapted to the peculiar needs of this industry, and embraces every known labor-saving device for the production of the mechanism of the clocks as well as the handsome cases enclosing them. And in this connection it might be mentioned that the engine and much of the machinery were designed and built by Mr. **Durphy, the superintendent,** before he had any idea of being connected with the concern, **and for the** substantial work then done he now has reason to congratulate himself.

Forty different styles and combinations are made by the Ithaca Calendar Clock Company, **and it** is not an unusual proceeding to make a clock to suit some **special room in** any wood or design that may be desired. Fourteen special calendar clocks were last year made for the State Capitol at Albany and the universal satisfaction given is proverbial. The New York office of the company is with the Waterbury Clock Company, at No. 4, Cortlandt street, and transactions with either this or the home office are attended with the most satisfactory results. **And** with the facilities possessed by the Ithaca Calendar Clock Company and a reputation extending from one end of the civilized world to the other, there need not any fear be expressed that competitors will outstrip them in the race for patronage, or Ithaca **fail to receive continued** benefits from the industry that has added so largely to its industrial reputation.

MARSH & HALL.

The **establishment** of which Messrs. John O. Marsh and Edwin M. Hall are the proprietors justly ranks as the foremost retail house in Tompkins county, and in some **important respects it equals, if** not excels, some of the largest stores in any of the **neighboring cities.** The fine business of which these gentlemen are to-day the **fortunate** possessors has been built up in the course of **twelve** years, entirely through the energy and mercantile sagacity of the present members of the firm. In **1871** Mr. Marsh, who had for a long term of years been engaged in trade in the near-by village of McLean, in connection with his brother, D. B. Marsh, sold his interests there and removed to **Ithaca.** Mr. Hall **entered** the co-partnership with Mr. Marsh, with a business experience of **seven years,** one of which was passed in the employ of the former firm **of** J. W. & J. Quigg, and **six** with Granger & Co. Marsh & Hall began the dry-goods business in the handsome **store at** 53 East State street. A fine trade was ere long established, and the **business** success of the new firm became an assured fact. In 1877 through the failure **of the firm occupying the spacious store in** the Wilgus Block at the corner of **Tioga and State streets it became vacant.** Several firms in succession had failed while occupying **this store, and when Marsh &** Hall announced their intention of removing their growing **business to** the more commodious quarters in the Wilgus Block, the wisdom of the proposed change was generally questioned by their many friends. However the change was made and the result has verified the soundness of judgment of the enterprising gentlemen, who scouting all thoughts of disaster, boldly enlarged their lines as favorable opportunity was presented. Their trade has been enlarged in six years to upwards of four times the dimensions it had attained in the store at first occupied. The value of the stock carried is now about $75,000 and the sales for the current year will exceed $150,000.

The business of this important firm occupies the first floor and basement of the Wilgus Block, the **dimensions of** each floor being 100x46 feet; a portion of the basement **of the adjoining store is also made use of.** The main floor consists of two divisions, the east one being devoted to the dry goods, clothing and fancy-goods and notion stock, and the west division, to a complete line of groceries, provisions, crockery, and glass ware.

The line of fine silks, and other rich dress goods carried is very large and varied. It is worthy of notice in passing that the sale of silks this year, has been the largest ever enjoyed by the firm, although they have made a specialty of silks for some years. The custom clothing department is an important one, a very large stock of suitings and overcoat cloths being carried. The feature of the business, however, in which Marsh & Hall easily outrank all other houses in this section of the State is in their carpet stock. The whole of the extensive floor age of the basement is devoted to this stock, which has frequently reached the value of from $25,000 to $28,000. It is a positive fact that one cannot find else where in this State, a place the size of Ithaca, in which so large, complete and varied a stock of carpets is kept as at this store, and it is said by well informed persons, that even the fine neighboring cities of Elmira, Binghamton and Auburn do not contain a store carrying a carpet stock equal to that of Marsh & Hall. This is an interesting and instructive item in the consideration of the mercantile resources of this village.

The several departments of this admirable store are in the charge of experienced, capable men, who are assisted by a corps of courteous and obliging salesmen. There are fifteen men employed in the several departments of the store. The existence here of this large, splendidly stocked, and finely conducted store, is a decided credit to this village, and the fact that it is prosperous, and its trade increasing yearly is an evidence of the large business capacity of its proprietors, as well as of the ability to properly appreciate mercantile enterprise and worth on the part of the residents of this village and the surrounding farming districts.

C. J. RUMSEY & CO.

One of the largest and most prosperous establishments conducted by a firm of young men in Ithaca is that of C. J. Rumsey & Co., situated at 68 East State street. For upwards of fifty years this store has been continuously occupied for the sale of hardware. Prior to that time a frame building stood upon the site of the present building in which a small theatre was conducted by the Atwaters. This building was destroyed by fire in 1832 or 1833. Then a brick building was erected on the site and was opened as a hardware store. This was conducted for years by the late George B. McCormick, and Jacob McCormick. Afterwards the store was managed by E. G. Pelton, who in 1858 sold the business to the late John Rumsey. By him it was conducted with large profit and success for thirty years. It is said that by a fortunate purchase of nails and spikes in large quantities just previous to the outbreak of the War of the Rebellion, Mr. Rumsey in consequence of the great increase in the price of iron during the following year realized from their sale, and his trade for the year in general, the sum of $30,000. This was the beginning of his subsequent very successful business career. In 1876, Charles J. Rumsey who had for a number of years been in the employ of John Rumsey, became a part owner of the business, the firm becoming John Rumsey & Co. In 1878 John Rumsey withdrew entirely from the business, and a copartnership was formed by C. J. Rumsey, Edwin Jillett, and Edgar M. Finch, under the style of C. J. Rumsey & Co. Mr. Finch wtthdrew from the firm a year later, and Messrs. Rumsey & Jillett have since continued the business under the same firm name. The large business which had been done in the earlier days of John Rumsey's sole proprietorship had somewhat depreciated toward the end of his mercantile career. The falling off in trade at this old and favorably known stand has been much more than made good however by the vigorous young firm now conducting it. The volume of trade for the current year will far exceed that of any previous year in the history of the store, when the fact is remembered that the prices now prevailing are very much lower than in former years.

The stock carried is an extensive and varied one, the large three story and basement building being filled to its entire capacity and part of a second building fronting on Tioga Street is also used. In addition to a full supply of stoves and ranges in all the principal leading styles, and general hardware, the firm deal extensively in fine pocket cutlery, carpenter's tools, bird cages, blacksmith's supplies, and sash, doors and blinds. There is a large tin shop connected with the store, where tinware of all kinds is manufactured, and in this department are several experienced roofers. Rumsey & Co. are agents for this section of the famous Hazard powder, a magazine where a large supply of powder is kept on hand having been erected by them a few years ago. In the several departments of the business twelve men are employed. Their fine prizes of "Happy Thought" ranges, given for the last two years to the handsomest child under two years of age shown at the fair of the Tompkins County Agricultural Society, have strongly attested the public spirit and enterprise of the firm, and the baby shows thus brought about have been among the leading features of the fairs. The confidence and esteem in which Mr. Rumsey is held by his fellow citizens was given public expression by his election last season to the Presidency of the village, an office whose complex duties he succeeds in discharging most acceptably to citizens generally without regard to their political affiliations. The members of this firm believe fully in the principle of letting the outside world know what they are doing and their fine and yearly increasing trade proves most clearly the wisdom of their course. They are also satisfied that what Ithaca needs most from a commercial point of view is the ecouragement of a movement for the enlargement of the manufacturing interests of the place, having sufficient business sagacity to plainly foresee that any increase of those interests will be necessarily accompanied by a corresponding growth and enlargement of the established mercantile trade of the place. Should this liberal sentiment fortunately continue to develop through the encouragement of President Rumsey and other equally progressive citizens, the future commercial importance of Ithaca may with good reason be expected to very considerably increase.

J. C. STOWELL & SON.

That Ithaca is fortunate in possessing a number of well-stocked and admirably managed retail groceries is a fact which has not unfrequently been alluded to in the public prints, but that there is also in existence here a wholesale grocery and provision store on an important scale and equal in many respects to large city establishments of a similar character is not so generally understood. A glance through the excellently appointed and fully stocked wholesale grocery and provision house of Messrs. J. C. Stowell & Son, on West State street, would convince the most skeptical of the truth of this statement. The fine business now transacted by this reliable and enterprising firm has had a growth extending through a long term of years. Its large increase during the last ten years, however, which has brought it into the front rank of the important commercial enterprises of this place, has in a large degree been made possible by the excellent transportation facilities and reduced rates, which have resulted from the admirable and popular conduct, by the Lehigh Valley Company, of its railroad reaching this village. In 1835 John C. Stowell, then a young man only 18 years of age came to this village from Groton, in this county, and entered the employ of Miles Finch, proprietor of a general merchandise store. Five years later by close attention to business and the strictest integrity he had so won the esteem of his employer that he was taken in as an equal partner, the firm becoming Finch & Stowell. The business prospered and after twelve years passed exclusively into the hands of the junior member of the firm. A little later S. P. Sherwood became associated with Mr. Stowell and the firm of Stowell & Sherwood continued until 1864. The general merchandise business was conducted by Mr. Stowell until 1872, when it was sold to H. L. Wilgus. Mr. Stowell, associating with himself, his son, Calvin D. Stowell, who was then a recent graduate of Yale, began a wholesale grocery and produce business in the old brick store adjoining his fine new block, which had previously been occupied by J. H. Hintermister for the manufacture of organs. In 1875 the business had prospered so well that the building occupied was found to be far too small. Then in connection with C. M. Titus, the Messrs. Stowell built the large, fine block, known as the Titus & Stowell block, which now ornaments West State street. In 1876 the new store was taken possession of, in addition to the former quarters, by Stowell & Son. The new store is a model of neatness and perfect fitness for the purposes to which it was designed. It consists of a large roomy basement, and four upper floors, 85x35 feet, all connected both by stairways and a large and admirably operating passenger and freight elevator, of the Reedy patent

In all the attributes of a first-class wholesale grocery, provision and retailer's supply house, the establishment of Messrs. Stowell & Son, is not surpassed in this section of the State. They are constantly adding to their reputation and mercantile importance through a system of strict reliability, and fair dealing. Mr. Stowell, in addition to his large commercial connections, is a director of the First National Bank, and was one of the incorporators. The important business which the Messrs. Stowell have succeeded by industry, enterprise and honest dealing in building up, will doubtless continue to grow, bringing credit to the place in which it is located, and further financial prosperity to the worthy proprietors.

HENRY BOOL.

A little more than ten years ago, while the splendid Cornell mansion which now graces East Hill was still in an unfinished condition, among the artisans employed there was a certain young Englishman, a carpenter and joiner who was working on "short hours". After spending a few months here the idea occurred to him to take up as a source of additional revenue the work of canvassing for subscribers for the New York weekly newspapers, viz: *The Independent* and the *Golden Age*. He seemed to possess peculiar qualifications for the work and much success attended his efforts in this direction. One evening while talking earnestly with a well-known merchant on State street in regard to subscribing for one of the above mentioned papers, ex-President Sisson, who was standing near and had overheard the conversation, turned to the young man, saying: "You ought to drop the jack plane altogether and make a steady business of canvassing." The advice conveyed in these words was shortly followed, and thereafter for a year or more, the quondam carpenter and joiner pushed vigorously his canvassing. From early morn until long after sundown he journeyed about, extending his travels into surrounding towns and villages and to the remotest borders of the county. The knowledge acquired in these visits to the homes of the well-to-do people of the county was to be in the future of great service to the young man, and the means saved from his year's work at canvassing, fortunately invested, formed the basis of much prosperity in years to come. The reader is asked to imagine a period of ten years gone by. A fine three story building comes to view. Through its beautiful plate glass front may be seen a profusion of rich and varied wares; up and down the spacious store move the many customers, and courteous salesmen and ladies are supplying their wants, or showing them about the establishment, which from basement to roof is literally packed with goods. New goods are being received, purchased wares sent out for delivery, busy sounds come from the large work shops at the rear, and moving quietly about directing the whole machinery of this, the largest and best stocked art, furniture and variety goods store in this section of the State, is a plainly dressed, hard-worked appearing man. This is the proprietor of the splendid place of business that has been briefly described. From the humblest beginnings this magnificent result has been achieved in the short space of ten years, and solely through the unfailing industry, frugality, business sagacity and enterprise of one man. For the quondam carpenter and joiner, who has been described as the persevering canvasser, of ten years ago, is none other than the successful merchant of to-day, Henry Bool. But a more detailed description of Mr. Bool's establishment and of its growth from so small a start to its present large proportions will be found interesting. As a canvasser in 1873 for subscribers to the *Independent* and *Golden Age*, Mr. Bool was often requested by his customers to have framed for them the premium pictures which the publishers of those newspapers were in the habit of sending out. It soon occurred to him that it would be profitable for him to make these frames himself. So he got small quarters in the Krum building, over what was then Uri Clark's jewelry store, now Sugarman's clothing store. Here for a year or more he worked in a small way, framing the pictures for subscribers, and gradually getting together a small stock of frames and pictures. In 1874 he bought the pictures, frames and fine art goods of Wood & Priest, who had several months previously begun business in the store under the Ithaca Hotel. Bool then removed to quarters over Miss Ackley's news and stationery store, then in the frame building

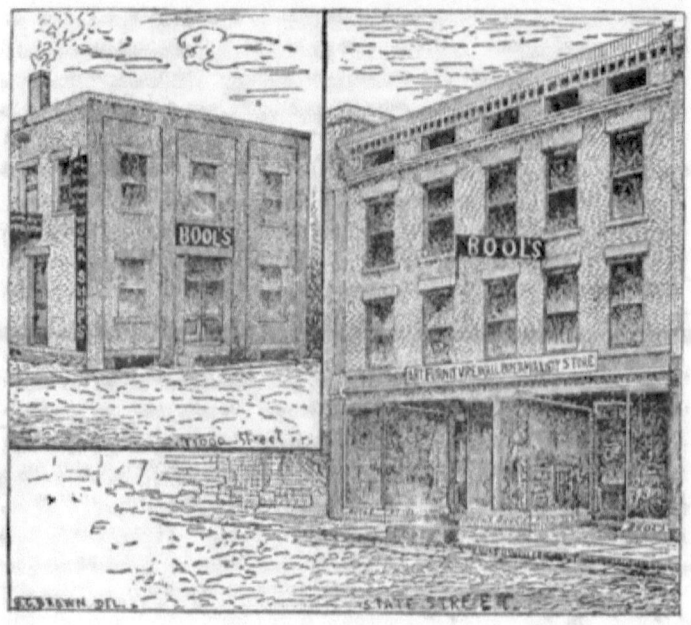

adjoining the County Clerk's office on Tioga street. In this place he remained for two years, his business constantly growing, until it became necessary to find more room elsewhere. In the spring of 1875 he removed to the store in the Pumpelly Block, now occupied by R. A. Heggie. His stock was greatly added to and after a year or two a new departure in the line of house furnishing goods was made. The business still continued to prosper although wiseacres shook their heads, and remarked that Bool was a hard worker and ought to succeed, but he was trying to grow too fast and disaster was sure to follow. He kept on persistently, however, tiding storms which threatened severely at times. The floor immediately over his store was soon secured, then successively the third floors of a number of adjoining buildings were found to be necessary, and still the growth did not cease. Finally about two years ago the ground floor of the Culver Block having become vacant, Mr. Bool, through the advice and encouragement of Mr. Geo. E. Priest, of the *Journal*, and by virtue as well of his own progressive and pushing spirit, concluded to make a still bolder move and take possession of that large store. He was openly laughed at by some business men for his presumption in daring to go into such a big store. One facetious person wanted to know if he would not plant a potato patch in one corner of the store to help fill it up. Mr. Bool nothing daunted made the change—and thanks to his vim and enterprise the venture has proved a wise one. From occupying the first floor and basement, he has come to be sole occupant of the block, which is 147 feet deep, 37 feet wide and possessed of three stories and basement. He also occupies what was known formerly as the "store house". This is a two story and basement building facing on South Tioga street. It is 70x33 feet, and connects at the rear with the main building which fronts on State street. The area of his floorage is upwards of 35,-

ooo square feet. The store presents a very attractive appearance with its beautiful full length plate **glass windows**, in which frequently changing and most elaborate displays of rich furniture, tapestry and household furnishing goods are made. The business carried on is very extensive and embraces a wide range of goods both in regard to **cost and use.** Here may be found elegant paintings and engravings, as well as art and artists' goods of all kinds; an extensive stock of furniture from the cheapest to the most expensive, wall paper, stationery, toys, crockery, **glass ware,** etc., etc. The manufacture of picture frames, window shades, and upholstered goods is carried on extensively. Thirteen men are employed in this department. In the store proper are twelve employes, making a total of twenty five employes at Mr. Bool's establishment. The value of the goods in **stock** is not less than $50,000. The average daily sales have constantly increased during the occupancy of the new **store, and** their aggregate for the current year will reach a very large sum. **The business growth of** Mr. Bool has been unparalleled in the history of commercial enterprises in this place, and he has the satisfaction of **knowing that he has compelled success** through hard work, enterprise and **business sagacity.**

HAWKINS, TODD & CO.

The oldest of the leading dry goods houses, the establishment **of Hawkins, Todd & Co.,** at No. 22 East State street, is deserving of more than a passing mention in ITHACA AND ITS RESOURCES. Thirty-one years ago **N. S.** Hawkins, then quite a young boy, came from Cayuga County to Ithaca to clerk in the **store of Avery, Woodworth & Co.,** at the time (1852) one of the largest stores in the village. He was **an industrious young man and a good** salesman, and when in 1861 a reorganization of the firm occurred he became one of the partners. The new firm of Morrison, Hawkins **& Co.** abandoned the sale of groceries, which formerly comprised a portion of the stock, **and** confined themselves **to dry goods exclusively.** They were very successful, **and** continued the business **until 1869,** when the firm was again reorganized under the title of Hawkins, Finch **& Co.** This firm continued with like success, and a couple of **years ago prepared to close out,having** acquired a competency and desiring rest. **Mr. Finch did retire, but in compliance** with the wishes of the two **young men, Messrs. L. G. Todd** and J. J. Rounseville,who were negotiating for the **purchase of the business, Mr. Hawkins** concluded to remain "in harness," and in the spring of 1883 the old house again **changed name,** the title becoming, this time, **Hawkins,** Todd & Co. Messrs. **Todd and Rounseville** had for ten years previously been the leading salesmen in the house of Marsh & Hall, and were both very popular, possessing a large circle of **friends and acquaintances.** Consequently when they entered this house in connection with Mr. **Hawkins,** who had been found in this same storeroom nearly every day from the time he entered it as a boy thirty-one years ago, the business took a sudden jump and began to increase rapidly. How this combination of enterprising young men with the head of so old and well established an house works may be inferred from the statement that the business has increased fully 100 per cent. since the firm **of** Hawkins, Todd **& Co.** was organized. A new life has been infused into it, **and** the stock **of** British, French, German and American Fancy and Staple Dry Goods which had been allowed to run down in anticipation of closing out, has not only been newly filled in but largely added to, and a larger or more elegant stock of these goods cannot now be found in Ithaca. A new departure made by the firm since its reorganization, and one that is appreciated by their customers, is merchant tailoring. A full line of cloths has always been carried, but in compliance with the request of a large number of Messrs. Todd and Rounseville's friends the firm undertook to "make up" these cloths, and the consequence is that a first class cutter and several men and women are now given employment in this branch of the business. And it might here be parenthetically mentioned that Ithaca and Oswego are the only places known where the dry goods and merchant tailoring business are combined, but it is claimed that Hawkins, Todd & Co. make gentlemen's clothing to order at one third less than suits of the same quality and workmanship cost in New York. Their large storeroom, 20 feet wide and 90 feet deep, in which seven people are constantly employed, is a representative mercantile establishment, and there can be no doubt but that the success which has marked the beginning of Hawkins, Todd & Co's. career as a firm will prove to have been only a harbinger of greater successes to come, and which will eclipse all previous efforts made to please and attract the public in this old and well-known storeroom.

ITHACA MANUFACTURING WORKS.

As a centre for both manufacture and commerce Ithaca certainly presents advantages that cannot be ignored by those seeking a suitable or desirable location for almost any branch of business, and the establishment of new enterprises in greater number within the past few years is evidence that this fact is becoming recognized. Indeed, the extent and diversity of its manufacturing and comcial interests, as shown in these pages, will doubtless surprise many residents of the village. A new era of prosperity seems to have set in. The success of the newer industries has been uniformly satisfactory, while the older industries, and those whose earlier years were fraught with much labor and little profit— with failure to realize the sanguine expectations of the promoters of the enterprise, have apparently begun an era of prosperity that is no more pleasing to their stockholders or owners than to the citizens at large, who see in their advancement and prosperity a corresponding increase in the advancement and prosperity of Ithaca. Among the latter class may be mentioned the Ithaca Manufacturing Works, and the fact that the capital employed in this concern is owned away from home, makes no less satisfactory the later success of this establishment, which under the name of Ithaca Agricultural Works, after a season of apparent prosperity, followed by failure and foreclosure, was succeeded by the Ithaca Manufacturing Works, has become a prosperous institution and is now profitably conducted. The Ithaca Agricultural Works were established on a small scale in 1867 for the manufacture of agricultural implements, principally a patent hay rake and a seeder, and so much confidence was felt in their merits that a company was formed and incorporated under this title to increase manufacturing and extend the business. The business did increase rapidly. Within four years a cluster of buildings on the bluff on the south side of Fall Creek had been erected, large numbers of these agricultural implements were annually produced and the company was apparently in the most prosperous condition. But the plan adopted in putting the product of the works on the market was not a proper one, and although apparently prosperous the works were constantly losing money. A natural culmination of this state of affairs was failure—the mortgages on the property were foreclosed and in 1879 the Ithaca Agricultural Works ceased to do business. The establishment was bought in by Mr. J. W. Hollenback, a wealthy coal land owner of WilkesBarre, Pa , and the holder of the mortgages. He sent an experienced man of business, Mr. J. E. Patterson, also of Wilkes-Barre, here to take charge of the works and continue the business. The title was now changed to the Ithaca Manufacturing Works, a new system was inaugurated and this industry has finally become a paying institution. The business has increased about 25 per cent each year since 1880 and the prospects are decidedly favorable for a steady prosperous business henceforth. Since October, 1881, the works have been managed by Messrs. P. H Pursel and J. A. Mortimore, but Mr. Pursel has lately been entrusted with the sole management of the concern and there need be no fear that the future of the industry will be any the less bright for being placed in his hands. Indeed, the Ithaca Manufacturing Works, with proper management could not fail to prove successful, for in location, facilities, &c., they possess every requisite to success. The location on Fall Creek bluff, with the great water power furnished by Ithaca Fall dam, is an exceptionally good one, while the buildings and plant are equal to the demands of a much greater production. The office and wareroom, No. 51 Lake street, occupy a two-story brick structure, 30x100 feet in dimensions ; the paint shop is a two story frame building, 30x60 feet ; the wood-working department is also a two story frame building, 42x65 feet ; the blacksmith shop is 28x30 feet ; and the foundry, which is across Tunnel Creek, and connected with the other buildings by a bridge 117 feet in length, is 30x60 feet in dimensions. These buildings, as well as a number of smaller ones and sheds, are all connected by a system of narrow-gauge railway, and are thoroughly equipped with every necessary tool and labor-saving invention for facilitating the rapid production of the specialties manufactured—the Leader Hay Rake and the Improved Tompkins County Cultivator. A working force of from 20 to 30 people are employed and about 2,000 rakes and 2,000 cultivators are now produced annually. The trade is largely in this State, but the demand for the rakes and cultivators also extends throughout the entire United States. Both the Leader Hay Rake and the Tompkins County Cultivator are acknowledged as being the most improved implements for their respective purposes manufactured, and the patents are owned by the Ithaca Manufacturing Works. It is said that no testimonials are required to sell them, their points of superiority being recognized by every intelligent farmer, and consequently there is little likelihood of the industry becoming of less, but every probability of its becoming of still greater value to Ithaca. The present manager, Mr. P. H. Pursel, has been connected with the works in various capacities since Mr. Hollenback took possession in 1879, and is well-fitted for the position both by the reason of the experience thus gained and his previous business experience. He is a native of Columbia County, Pa., but for a number of years before coming to Ithaca was a trusted employe of the Miners' Savings Bank and other prominent establishments in WilkesBarre, Pa., and it is confidently asserted that under his management the Ithaca Manufacturing Works will not only retain the position it has so lately gained, but advance still farther and ultimately become what it was so fondly hoped in its earlier years it would become—one of the largest industries in Ithaca.

URI CLARK.

The name which heads this sketch is that of one of the successful self-made business men of Ithaca. Thirty-one years ago, as a young boy Uri Clark entered the old established jewelry store of Joseph Burritt, to learn the trade. As an apprentice and expert jeweler the young man remained in Mr. Burritt's employ for twelve years. In 1864 he became a part owner in the business under the firm name of Burritt, Clark & Co. A year later he disposed of his interest in the business to enter the service of Uncle Sam, as first lieutenant of Co. L. of the 58th N. Y. S. V. The war fortunately coming to a close three months later, his company came back from Elmira where it had been stationed. Then he again entered the jewelry business and has since uninterruptedly pursued it with large success. From a store on East State street, which Mr. Clark opened on returning from Elmira, in 1867, he removed to the Krum building at the corner of State and Tioga streets. At this stand, where he remained for thirteen years, Mr. Clark was successful in building up a very large trade. During these successful and prosperous years Mr. Clark gave to his work the closest and most unremitting attention, and was repaid by large commercial prosperity. In 1880 he purchased and greatly improved the building at 36 East State street. The store was handsomely remodeled, provided with a fine plate glass front, and marble floor, and in all respects admirably appointed for the purpose of a jewelery store. Since Mr. Clark's occupancy of his present handsome store he has not, it is true, given to business his whole time and energies as was the case in earlier years. Relaxation from the incessant cares and wearing work of former years have been obtained in the pleasure of yachting and residence on the shores of the beautiful lake near at hand, Mr. Clark having several years ago purchased a fine steam yacht, and caused to be erected on the west shore of Cayuga, a charming summer cottage. But nevertheless under his experienced personal supervision, his store has continued to enjoy its high standing, and a fair proportion of the best class of patronage. Mr. Clark is known as one of the most expert lapidaries in the trade in this portion of the State, and in his cases are to be found many beautiful and costly gems in rare and attractive settings. A large line of optical goods is kept on hand, and glasses are selected for all kinds of impaired vision with the utmost care and precision. In addition to a full and complete line of goods properly belonging to the business, Mr. Clark's store contains a splendid stock of sporting goods, including fine rifles, shot guns, shells and reloading apparatus, ammunition, game bags, fine fishing rods, tackle, flies and all articles of the kind. Along with his success in business matters, Mr. Clark has also gained a reputation for uprightness and integrity which is known to all. He has been the firm friend of all movements looking to the commercial improvement of the place, the increasing of its educational advantages, and upholding of the good order and moral well being of the community. As explaining a title by which Mr. Clark is generally known to his friends and neighbors, it may be said that while connected with the recently disbanded 50th Battalion, he was made a Colonel on the staff of General Blood, commanding the 28th Brigade. To conclude this little sketch it is only fitting to say that the career of Col. Clark, who is in the very prime of life, with business success attained and enjoying in a high degree the respect and good will of his neighbors and fellow-townsmen, forms a striking illustration of the oft quoted and much doubted, yet still perfectly true, saying, that industry and honesty will surely bring success.

ITHACA GUN WORKS.

A new industry just started, and one which must prove of the greatest value to Ithaca, is the manufacture of breech-loading shot guns for sportsmen. The fact that between 170,000 and 200,000 guns are annually imported into the United States is of itself sufficient reason why such an industry should be started with bright hopes of success, but when that industry begins by producing a gun in every way the equal of the best sportsmen's fowling-piece manufactured, and at one-third less the cost, then hopes of success turn into certainty of success. And such may be said to be the prospects of the Ithaca Gun Works, which have just been put in operation. The price of a Parker and other first class breech-loading shot guns has always been an insurmountable objection to their purchase by a great number of sportsmen. As a gunsmith and inventor of high ability, W. H. Baker attained a wide reputation a few years since for the invention of the now celebrated Baker double and three barrel guns. While engaged in perfecting this gun he conceived the idea of producing a gun which, while possessing the very best shooting qualities, and being the equal in every respect of the Parker and other choice guns, from the simplicity of its mechanism could be manufactured and sold at much less than could other guns of the same quality. He worked on this idea until he had perfected a gun that not only convinced him of the correctness of his original ideas, but that it could command a large share of the patronage now going to importers of the guns made in Europe as well as occupy the same position in the eyes of sportsmen as the Parker, while it could be sold at one-third less. Messrs. D. McIntyre and J. E. VanNatta, of Ithaca, were then interested in this new invention, and as a result the gun was patented and last February a copartnership was formed between Messrs. Baker, McIntyre and VanNatta to manufacture under the title of the Ithaca Gun Works. Early in the present year the property at Fall Creek lately occupied by the bending works was purchased and during the entire summer work has been progressing on the special machinery required to make the plant complete. The buildings being properly fitted up, manufacturing was lately begun and the Ithaca Gun Works now have a plant with a capacity for producing ten guns per day. In securing this location for their works they have been very fortunate. The power furnished by Fall Creek is sufficient for a factory three times as large, and as they own both the sixth and seventh water privileges on the creek, the former affording 40 and the latter 60-horse power, they are prepared for any emergency. The main building of the works is 40x50 feet in dimensions, two stories, with an L 30x40 feet. There are also a forge shop 20x30 feet, and other necessary buildings. Both the main building and forge shop are equipped with the most improved tools, and most of the machinery in the works is of a special character and has been made on the premises. With this new and complete plant the Ithaca Gun Works are enabled to produce a gun that must take the same place in sportsmen's favor as the Parker; and at the same time cost about one-third less. The "Ithaca" gun, for that is the name of the new invention, contains all the standard points called for in a gun of the first quality, such as the Stop Lever Action, Rebounding Lock, Low Hammers, and Patent Compensating Fore-end, but there are less than half the parts in its mechanism than are usually employed to produce the same results. These few parts are all contained in the breechpiece, which is one solid piece of wrought iron, and all the parts, too, are made perfectly interchangeable. The simplicity of construction is a feature that will be appreciated by every sportsmen, while the style and finish of the "Ithaca" gun is equal to the Parker, Colt, Peiper or any other first-class gun—in fact, it is claimed to be the simplest and best gun manufactured in the world. Being an entirely new model, and possessing points of merit that are readily perceived by the sportsman or gundealer, and withal being sold at one-third the price charged for other first-class guns, great popularity may be anticipated for the new "Ithaca." Mr. W. H. Baker, the inventor, personally superintends their manufacture, and his large experience as a gunsmith and reputation as an inventor, will be a sufficient guarantee of the quality and workmanship that may be expected. Both the other members of the firm, Messrs. D. McIntyre and J. E. VanNatta, are practical men and inventors in their lines of business, and the management of the new concern will doubtless be characterized by a wise policy that will make their auspicious beginning only a forerunner of the great success to follow.

THE WEST END DRUG STORE.

A host of interesting associations and recollections cluster around the record of this, the oldest existing drug house in Ithaca, and, in fact, with but a single exception, the earliest established drug business in the community. As nearly as can be ascertained the first drug business established here was that of Mr. Miller, who had a small store on the site of the present Sprague Block. This business was begun very early in the century. In the employ of Mr. Miller was B. S. Halsey, now living and over eighty years of age. Mr. Halsey was the founder of the West End Drug Store. The building at 6 East State street, which continually for 51 years has been occupied for a drug store, was built about 1822 by Horace Mack, and occupied by him until 1832 as a dry goods store. It was then taken possession of by B. S. Halsey and fitted up as a drug store. During the more than half a century since the business was established by Mr. Halsey, it has had a career full of incident and change. It has passed successively through the hands of eleven firms and individual owners. Sometimes the volume of trade enjoyed was large, and at others it was much reduced, but in spite of all the vicissitudes of its extended history, it has attained a vigorous and honourable old age. Following Mr. Halsey, in the order of their proprietorship came Dr. Webster, P. C. Schuyler, G. W. Schuyler, Dr. A. H. Monell, William Monell, Monell & Lawrence, J. Y. Lawrence, Tolfree & Mandeville, W. S. Mandeville, H. I. Smith, and lastly the present owners, Haskin & Todd. Although the business of the West End Drug Store has been at times in the hands of very capable and enterprising men, as will appear from the names which have been mentioned, and by some of them has been made the source of much business prominence and commercial prosperity, still it has perhaps become better known, and is accorded a more extensive patronage under its present proprietors than at any previous period of its long career. Something over two years ago, the business was purchased of H. I. Smith by Hiram L. Haskin and Judson B. Todd. Both of these young men entered upon the business with a practical knowledge of it, acquired in the employment of a well-known drug firm of this village. Added to their practical acquaintance with the business, they possessed unusual energy, sagacity and a strong determination to win success. Their efforts have met with generous appreciation at the hands of the public, and to-day the West End drug store occupies a leading position not only in its especial line in this county, but ranks well up among the most successful retail business enterprises generally of this vicinity. During the two years' proprietorship of Messrs. Haskin & Todd, the stock has been very largely added to, and improved, the exterior and interior of the building have been materially altered for the better, and the firm has won a host of friends by its liberality and enterprise, as well as an enviable reputation for thorough reliability, and sound commercial credit, both at home and among wholesale dealers and manufacturers. For two years Haskin & Todd alone, of the several drug firms of Ithaca, made very fine displays at the large fair of the County Agricultural Society, their exhibit at the fair this season proving by far one of the most attractive features of Floral Hall, and arousing the warm admiration of the thousands visiting the exhibition.

The store is a very attractive one, containing a large and expensive soda-fountain, unusually large and handsome show cases, and fine fittings generally. With an excellent stand, a large and varied stock, a wide and rapidly growing business acquaintance and personal popularity, possessing ample means, undoubted credit, and an unswerving determination to retain and augment their fine trade by close attention to the wants of the public, and equal promptness in measures to meet them, and last, but not at all least, a full knowledge of the efficacy of the value of printer's ink properly applied, the young proprietors of the West End Drug Store can confidently look forward to a successful business career.

JACKSON & BUSH.

Within the last five years a great change has taken place in the dry goods trade in Ithaca. Previous to 1878 it was customary for the ladies desiring the finer qualities of dress goods to go to the larger cities to make their selections. Now there are to be found here as fine lines of these goods as can be purchased anywhere. What has worked this revolution, do you ask? Competition, forced by example. Five years ago a new firm came into Ithaca. They secured one of the finest store rooms in the place and opened a stock of the finer qualities of goods. Not only this, but the system of strictly one price was adopted and particular attention was paid to the comfort and convenience of their customers. As a result their store became the centre of attraction for lady shoppers, and their competitors were forced to sort up their stocks and also carry a finer line of goods. And they and their customers have been benefited thereby. The firm that may be credited with bringing about this desirable change is Jackson & Bush, whose handsome store-room, at No 53 East State street, is the favorite shopping place of the ladies in Tompkins County. With ten years' experience as a firm in the dry goods trade at Niagara Falls, they came to Ithaca in 1878, and immediately took the lead in their particular branch of business. They forced a competition from which the people derived the greatest benefit, and their reward has been in accord with their merits. Twice have they been compelled to enlarge their store, and their business has fully tripled in these five years. Now they have the largest and finest dry goods salesroom in the village, and one too, that would do credit to the largest cities. It is 25 feet wide and 120 feet deep, with high ceiling, and well lighted by side windows and skylights. The room is heated by steam furnished by a self-regulating boiler situated in the basement, and everything that can add to the comfort and convenience of the patrons has been furnished. Particularly is this noticeable in the arrangement of the rear portion of the store, which has been tastily carpeted and fitted up for the display of silks and ladies wraps, a specialty of the house. A ladies' toilet room is among the other conveniences that are here noticeable. The stock is judiciously arranged in departments ; here notions, there domestic dry goods ; foreign dress goods of the finest quality, ladies' furnishings, gents' furnishings, ladies' wraps, etc., all having their particular place and presenting as fine a display as one would expect to see in the bazaars of the East, of which such attractive descriptions have been written. The entire basement is occupied for the storage of duplicate stock, and the visitor is impressed with the fact that henceforth it is unnecessary to make expensive trips to distant cities for the purpose of purchasing the finer qualities of goods. As in the other dry goods houses, here, too, the making of gentlemen's clothing to order is one of the specialties, and it may well be said that a more elegant stock of suitings and trimmings cannot be found in any store in the State. And as of gentlemen's suitings, so it may be said of ladies' wear - from the cheapest to the very finest qualities of goods manufactured are presented for the inspection and selection of the visitor. Ten people are employed in the house, and in securing their assistants the firm have been extremely fortunate—in securing people who take so great an interest in the success of their house and who are so successful in pleasing the patrons of the establishment. In a word, here is a model dry goods store and one which cannot be otherwise than successful. Jackson & Bush have proven their ability to conduct profitably a first class establishment in this place, and their success has been the means of conferring many benefits upon the residents of Ithaca and this vicinity.

THE CLINTON HOUSE.

The most popular hotel in Ithaca, the Clinton House has a history which, could it be fully presented, would prove one of the most interesting parts of this little book. The building was erected between the years 1828 and 1831, but it still remains—with its massive columns supporting the broad porticos, the proportioned rise of the whole building, the belvidere crowning all—the most imposing and dignified building in all this beautiful plain. It was built by Henry Ackley,

Henry Hibbard and J. S. Beebe, and originally cost only $22,000—the builder of to day, however, would look with scorn upon an offer to erect such a building for this sum. In 1862 many internal and a few external modifications were made, but the reputation of the house has never changed. From its opening day down to the present time it has enjoyed the repute of being one of the best first-class hotels in the State. "The record of the house includes statesmen and jurists and the travelers of celebrity who have traversed the regions of Cayuga. From the venerable Surveyor-General DeWitt (the friend and correspondent of Washington), who watched its building with so much hope of its success, its register has been graced by thousands of names, good and true, not the least interesting page in which is that which records the signatures of the principal diplomats accredited to our government who in 1863 accompanied Mr. Seward, the Secretary of State, on a tour through this country." This was in the long ago, but the time intervening has only been a repetition of the story. Hotel-keeping has been the main occupation of the life of its proprietor—Sewall D. Thompson—and the thirty-three years he has presided over the Clinton House have served to establish his reputation as a model "Boniface". He was born in the town of Hubbardston, Mass., in 1809 and embarked in this avocation at the age of twenty-three by keeping a hotel at Athol, Mass., which he continued until 1837. After a brief stay in New York City he then came to Ithaca in the spring of 1838, and leased the Ithaca Hotel, which he managed until the fall of 1846. He then spent four years in mercantile pursuits in New York City and in 1850 returned to Ithaca and leased the Clinton House for a term of fifteen years, before the expiration of which, however, he purchased of Miss Beebe, a daughter of J. S. Beebe, one of the three owners, a third interest in the hotel property. In 1864 Ezra Cornell purchased the remaining two-thirds, and thorough repairs were then made, the hotel being closed for a year while the alterations and improvements were in progress. In 1865 the house was again opened under Mr. Thompson's management and conducted with great success ever since. He subsequently became sole owner, and his management of this hotel alone now counts up thirty-three years. He is one of the oldest hotel-keepers in the country, being now in his seventy-fourth year, but he is still hale and hearty and more active than most men at fifty. Mr. Thompson is now ably assisted in the management by his adopted son, Sewall D. Thompson, Jr., and it is not at all likely that the characteristics of the Clinton House— its home-like, comfortable qualities and the excellence of its *cuisine*—will ever be lost, for it is probable that it will remain under the control of a Thompson for many years to come, and that will be a sufficient guarantee of its general excellence and character.

H. V. BOSTWICK.

The extensive cooperage business of Hermon V. Bostwick, whose works are located on Clinton street, a short distance east of Cayuga street, is the only concern of its kind in Ithaca. The business was established originally in 1867. In the spring of 1873 the factory was destroyed by fire. Rallying quickly from this misfortune, Mr. Bostwick caused the shops to be rebuilt on a larger scale and by virtue of his energy and persistence has succeeded in building up a large trade. Twenty-five employes find occupation at these works and from one to two thousand cords of wood are worked up each year. The products of the factory include barrels, firkins and general cooperage. The quality of these wares is widely known and admitted throughout this section of the state and their sale reaches into every town of Tompkins county and several surrounding counties as well. In the manufacturing resources of the place the cooperage works of Mr. Bostwick occupy an important standing on account of their extent and the superiority of the products of his factory.

GEORGE SMALL.

Another illustration of success won by indomitable pluck and energy is furnished by the subject of this brief sketch. George Small came from England to this country when quite a young boy and settled in Ithaca. By dint of hard work he secured for himself the advantages of a good education, and overcoming obstacles that had proved too great for many a man, advanced step by step until he was able in 1876 to purchase the lumber business at the corner of Tioga and Green streets which had been established in 1871 by Howell & VanHouter. The business had changed hands several times before he purchased it, but under his management increased largely and became profitable. In 1881 he erected the three story brick building 63x48 in dimensions on the southwest corner of Tioga and Green streets, and put in machinery for matching and planing the lumber he sold. He now handles annually about 3,000,000 feet of lumber and gives employment to 10 or 12 men constantly. Two spacious lumber yards are owned by him, the one on the east side of Tioga street being 200x100 feet in dimensions and the other on the west side, being 132x160 feet. He has a large local retail trade and is doing a prosperous business. It is not with the intention of flattering Mr. Small, who is still quite a young man, that mention has thus briefly been made of the circumstances attending his rise by his own exertions to the honorable position he now occupies in this community, but as such examples not infrequently give courage to young men who are struggling along and now and then meeting with obstacles seemingly insurmountable and which almost crush out their ambition, it is thought that such facts come within the province of a work of this character, and they are accordingly noted with the hope that they will serve the purpose contemplated.

A. B. WOOD.

Among many other ways in which the existence of Cornell University in Ithaca has favorably affected the community, it has by virtue of its excellently conducted department of architecture given to the place several devotees to this line of effort, whose good taste and skillful training have been the means of developing better ideas among master-builders, artisans and the people of this village and vicinity generally in regard to the building of houses, business places and public structures. The many attractive residences erected here in later years, the considerable improvement in appearance of many of the village stores, and the much better taste shown even in the building of the commoner houses, sufficiently attest the truth of this statement. The gentleman whose name appears at the head of this article is among those who are to be credited with good service in this work. A. B. Wood, after devoting himself for several years to the study of architecture and associated branches at the University entered the practice in 1875. His office was with Allen Gray, insurance agent, in the Bates Block. While building up a patronage in his special line, Mr. Wood also found opportunity to acquaint himself with the details of insurance underwriting. In 1880 he became a partner of Mr. Gray in his extensive insurance business, and since the appointment of that gentleman as State agent for the Lorillard Insurance Company, something over a year ago, has had full charge of the local office. Mr. Wood has been the architect of not a few fine structures. Several admirable depot buildings have been erected for the Lehigh Valley Railroad Company, the most notable of which is the recently completed depot at WilkesBarre, Pa. The parochial school now building on West Buffalo street in this village is the design of Mr. Wood and promises to reflect much credit upon the architect. A number of the attractive new houses of Ithaca are the "children of his brain," the handsome house of Captain J. W. Tibbetts on West State street, being the chief example of Mr. Wood's ability in this line of architectural work. In the elements of convenience, substantiality, safety, and thorough sanitary precautions, Mr. Wood's buildings are not surpassed by the work of any of his business compeers of this section of the State. An element of character of this young man is thoroughness. This appears in his capacity as an underwriter, as well as in his other lines of effort. As a mark of the confidence of his insurance associates, it may be stated that at the reorganization of a local board in 1881 Mr. Wood was made secretary and treasurer of the board, and was again reappointed to the same office at the recent annual meeting.

DR. F. S. HOWE.

In 1872, Dr. F. S. Howe removed to Ithaca from the neighboring village of Dryden, where for sixteen years he had been engaged in the successful practice of dentistry. During the eleven years of his residence in this place Dr. Howe has greatly added to the fine reputation which he early won, as an unusually skillful operator in his branch of professional work, and has built up an excellent and widely extended patronage. The early training of Dr. Howe in the delicate and exceedingly important branch of dental work required in the operations connected with filling, in all its departments, was received with Dr. Benjamin Baker, for twenty years past a celebrated dental surgeon of Chicago, Ill., who formerly conducted an office in St. Louis, Mo. After mastering this class of operations, Dr. Howe was for a time with Dr. Luman Matson, then, as now, a successful dentist at Auburn, who is very proficient in the department of plate work. This thorough training, supplementing many superior natural qualifications possessed by Dr. Howe, gave him an easy road to the confidence and patronage of the public, when he entered formally upon his professional career. On first coming to Ithaca, Dr. Howe located in an office in the Andrus & Church block. In 1873 he removed to the fine quarters in the Bates block, which he has since continued to occupy. His patronage has rapidly grown, and his office has come to be widely known as one of the best equipped in all respects, and most ably conducted dental establishments in this section of the State. With all the care and responsibility of increasing business, Dr. Howe has still found time and opportunity to keep up with the rapid progress made in late years, in the art he practices. He has made frequent trips to the metropolis, for special study in certain lines of work, in the offices of the leading dental surgeons, and has, indeed, but very recently returned from a journey to New York, made for this purpose. Therefore he is fully abreast of the times, in his practical knowledge of all the improved process and apparatus known in the art of dentistry. All classes of work, or any particular kind of operation desired, can be performed at this establishment, in a scientific and satisfactory manner. In the branch of plate work, Dr. Howe's office doubtless leads all rivals in this part of the State. Dr. Howe, in addition to his successful pursuit of his professional occupation, has had no small success in musical achievement. He organized the Fiftieth Band, and was for a time, its efficient leader, withdrawing from its direction, owing to a multiplicity of other engagements. He has been for the past eleven years the leader of the Aurora street M. E. Church choir, and has had an important part in most of the larger musical affairs of this place.

R. C. CHRISTIANCE.

The foundations of the fine business now conducted at 66 and 68 East State street, by Ralph C. Christiance, were laid in 1846, when Cornelius Christiance, father of the present proprietor, opened a small retail boot and shoe store just across the street in the store now occupied by Theodore Dobrin. The business prospered under the direction of Mr. Christiance, who was a careful, prudent man. In 1861 the business was transferred to its present quarters, R. C. Christiance sometime previous to the removal having become a part owner. At the death of Cornelius Christiance in 1876, R. C. Christiance succeeded to the sole ownership of the business, and has been successful in largely increasing it and adding to its commercial importance. In addition to the fine retail trade in boots and shoes and large business in fine custom work, a considerable retail and wholesale business in trunks and satchels, and rubber goods has been built up. Eleven persons are employed in the establishment. The stock carried is large, the three story and basement building occupied by the business being packed with goods. Mr. Christiance has shown much shrewdness and sound judgment in the purchase and handling of rubber goods, and has realized handsomely from his operations in that line. In addition to the large quantities of this sort of goods received and disposed of from the store, very many orders are sent in to be filled from the factory. In a quiet, unassuming way, and through force of unusual business energy and sagacity Mr. Christiance has developed the trade established by his father, into one of the most important commercial enterprises of the place, his sales for the current year promising to reach fully $175,000. Mr. Christiance's thoroughness in any matter he engages in is well shown by his rapid growth in Masonry. From the humblest position in the ranks of this great body in a few years he pushed his way to the very fore-front. For several years he has held the important and responsible position of Grand Treasurer of the Grand Commandery of the State of New York. In all respects R. C. Christiance is one of the leading, representative business men of Ithaca.

WORTMAN & SON.

The business career of Jacob R. Wortman, the head of this well-known and prosperous firm, began in 1859, when in connection with George Breitenbecker, he opened a small meat market in the Clinton block on North Cayuga street. The venture did not prove a successful one, and after a time was abandoned. In 1865 Mr. Wortman took possession of the store at 16 North Aurora street, where he has remained during the succeeding eighteen years. Under his personal direction his business has prospered finely, and his market is recognized as the leading one in the place. In 1879 Mr. Wortman associated with him his son, L. S. Wortman, by whom he is ably seconded in his efforts to properly meet the demands of his large and growing trade. While Mr. Wortman has, through persistent industry and the possession of special qualifications for the business, been successful in building up a fine reputation in his line and a large patronage, he has also found time and inclination to interest himself in the general welfare of the community. In 1874 he was elected to a commissionership in the board of education, succeeding in that body the late John Gauntlett. He is still a member of the School Board, having been twice re-elected, and has, during the nine years of service in that capacity, been one of the most faithful, competent members, in all cases favoring in a prudent and conservative, but thoroughly earnest manner, projects which have tended to build up the schools of this village. In 1882 Mr. Wortman was elected one of the trustees of the village from the Second Ward, and in his capacity as a member of the village board, has found larger scope for the exercise of the business-like methods and wide-awake spiritedness of which he is the possessor in no small measure. As illustrating the fore-thought of the subject of this sketch, it is of interest to note that some years ago he purchased a farm of fifty acres situated along the lake front just south of McKinney's. This property has much increased in value since, and there is good prospect that at no very distant day, the whole lake front lying between McKinney's and the Corner-of-the-lake, will be in lively demand as sites for the many summer residences which Mr. Wortman and other progressive-minded citizens confidently anticipate will be erected. Surely there is no more healthy and charming location for the building of a summer cottage, or permanent dwelling, where large and attractive grounds could be had, possessing a host of natural points of beauty and desirableness, than this to which allusion has been made. Speed the day when, beginning with the Renwick property, than which there is no more eligible and charming place in the State for the establishing of a beautiful country home, surrounded by grounds which with slight improvement could not be surpassed anywhere, the whole eastern slope of Cayuga, running north for three miles at least, shall be adorned with the homes of the future well-to-do manufacturers and enterprising tradesmen of the revived Ithaca.

C. H. VAN HOUTER.

A very successful business enterprise, which has been built up in a comparatively few years by one of the young business men of the place, is the wholesale and retail lumber concern of C. H. Van Houter, located at the corner of Clinton and Cayuga streets. Peter Van Houter for years owned and operated a lumber yard on South Tioga street and his son, C. H. VanHouter, therefore grew up to a knowledge of the business, with which he is thoroughly acquainted in all its details. In 1875 he entered into a co-partnership with George Small and for three years this firm carried on the business now conducted by Mr. Small alone. In 1878 Mr. Van Houter opened a yard on his own account on the site of the brick planing mill at the corner of Green and Tioga streets. In 1880 he removed his growing business to its present location, where it has prospered well. From the dimensions of a limited retail trade the business has been greatly extended, and frequent shipments are made to Watkins, Geneva, Lyons, Auburn, and many other points within a radius of 50 miles. Orders have also been received from New York, points in New Jersey, and even in some instances from Boston. This yard is fully stocked in all respects, and a low range of prices is maintained. In some particular grades of lumber, Mr. Van Houter has been able to defy the competition of the largest wholesale dealers. A speciality is made of cut shingles, of which class of wares, a larger sale is made at this yard than by any other dealer in the State east of Buffalo and Tonawanda.

J. F. BRUEN.

The establishment in Ithaca of a large and fine store this season, devoted to the exclusive sale of carpets, rugs, oil cloths, and linoleum goods, excited considerable attention and interest. The premises occupied are located in the Rumsey block on North Tioga street, in the store formerly occupied by Spence Spencer, for the sale of books and stationery. Mr. Bruen, the proprietor, is a member of the firm of Bruen Brothers, large wholesale carpet dealers of New York, whose commercial reputation is of the highest standing. Having been for years a traveling salesman for the house, Mr. Bruen became at length desirous of locating permanently, and making a settled abiding place for himself and family. After tooking carefully over the field, he fixed upon **Ithaca** as a desirable place to live in, **and one that promised to** permit **the building** up in time a good trade. Accordingly the store in question was taken, **and after it** had been completely renovated and finely re-fitted, a splendid stock of carpets, rugs, curtains, oil cloths and linoleum goods was put in, and the place opened for public patronage. Mr. Bruen has pursued from the outset a very liberal method of proclaiming his establishment in our midst; attractive announcements appeared in the newspapers, large quantities of neat oil cloth school bags were distributed among the hundreds of children of the town, a very handsome display of rich carpets, rugs, etc. was made at the fine fair of the Agricultural Society in September, a fine carpet was presented to Torrent Hose Co. No. 5, for sale at their recent benefit fair, and in many varying ways the liberality of the firm has been displayed, and the way paved for a large and growing trade and popularity. Meanwhile business has grown and and considerable sales have already been made. There is room here for such men as J. F. Bruen, and his business should bring large financial prosperity.

R. A. HEGGIE.

The successful and growing jewelry and engraving business of which R. A. Heggie is the proprietor, located in a handsome, plate glass front store at 40 East State street, had its beginning in 1875, when Mr. Heggie, after a thorough practical training in the trade, made his first venture on his own account by leasing a portion of the book-store then conducted in the Rumsey Block on North Tioga street by **Spence Spencer.** Mr. Heggie's unusual skill as a designer and maker of **pins and badges, and as an engraver,** has won for him much more than a local reputation. Soon after his establishment here he began to receive considerable orders for fraternity pins, and during the eight years he has been in business has made a very large number, many of them being very handsome in design and unexcelled in the skillful workmanship displayed in their construction. As an engraver Mr. Heggie has no superior in this locality. In 1881 he removed his business to its present location, where it has prospered very finely. The store is neatly appointed in all respects, and its attractive cases contain **a handsome display of** fine diamonds, rich jewelry, watches, silverware, and gold pens. **The exhibit of fine jewelry,** diamonds and watches made by Mr. Heggie at the fair **of the Tompkins County Agricultural Society this fall** attracted **much admiration and received the premium awarded** by the society for superior merit.

WHITE & BURDICK.

Away back in Ithaca's history nearly every store carried a line of drugs, and and it was not until 1820 that the first drug store exclusively was established. A Dr. Miller was the pioneer in this branch of business, and there are living today here a few people who remember his drug store with its wonder-inspiring colored lights in the window, which stood on the present site of the ornate Sprague Block. Benjamin Halsey was a clerk in Dr. Miller's establishment, and succeeded him as the proprietor. For full forty years the drug business was carried on by Mr. Halsey and his son in different locations on State street. They were succeeded by J. Colwell, and in 1867 this old established business was purchased by Messrs. Charles H. White and D. W. Burdick. In 1860 the building No. 16 East State street was erected, and soon after the storeroom now occupied by Messrs. White & Burdick was secured as being a favorable location for this drug business. This firm have been very successful and have built up a large and profitable business. Their storeroom is 18 feet wide and 84 feet deep, with a large basement occupied for storage purpose. The business which, when originally started did not amount to more than that now usually done by some physician, has grown to proportions which would then have been considered extraordinarily large, and forms an excellent illustration of Ithaca's growth and progress in general.

THE PATRICK WALL SHOE STORE.

The business, located at No. 12 North Aurora street, of which the well-known boot and shoe merchant, Patrick Wall is in charge, was established by him in 1871 in a small store on South Aurora street. It was removed a year or two later to its present more attractive and commodious quarters, where is to be found a large and fine stock of boots and shoes, slippers and rubbers in all grades and at fair prices. The reputation of this well and favorably known house for honest dealing is excellent, and entitles it to the liberal patronage of Ithaca and vicinity.

THE AUTOPHONE COMPANY.

Within the last few years public attention has largely been drawn to automatic musical instruments, through the efforts of men of acknowledged genius and ability to perfect an instrument that, unlike the much execrated hand organ or more desirable music-box even, would produce all the latest music of the day as well as possess the range to give the variety of the costly organ or piano, without requiring the skill and the ability requisite to the performance on those instruments. While almost every person is attracted and pleased, more or less, by music, there are comparatively few who can master the trained ear or facility of execution necessary to success—to render correctly the simpler melodies even, let alone the grand conceptions of the masters—and that there is a demand for such instruments has been conclusively proven by the avidity with which the public have purchased the results of every attempt in this direction, however crude. Various degrees of success have attended the efforts of those who have attempted to produce such an instrument, and the country has been literally flooded with their inventions, most of which are awkward and complicated, lacking in both simplicity and economy and giving very imperfect and unsatisfactory results. Among those who engaged in the attempt was Mr. H. B. Horton, of Ithaca, whose genius and ability are well known. After working several years on the problem, he was finally rewarded for his perseverance with its satisfactory solution, and produced as the result, the Autophone, which is now so widely and favorably known as the most perfect and desirable automatic musical instrument ever invented. The Autophone possesses many points of advantage over all other automatic musical instruments in elegance, utility, simplicity of construction, economy and execution, but chiefly in its music, the condensation of the music allowing a greater number of notes and consequently more harmony. Unlike the others, too, the feed of the music is intermittent, being controlled by a simple piece of mechanism forming one of the features of the patent, and the regularity and perfection with which the music is rendered is remarkable. The vast range of music it is capable of rendering embraces not only the sacred and instrumental music commonly known, and the popular songs of the day, but the more difficult and classical compositions which only the professional artists perform, as well as the operas. The instruments are manufactured of the very best materials and finished in styles both unique and handsome, making them a decided ornament in any household, while their durability is such that with reasonable care they will last a long time, and even if from any cause they become out of tune the reeds can be detached, returned to the factory and re-tuned at a very slight cost. They are not toys, but substantial musical instruments of remarkable power, sweetness and purity of tone, capable of spreading delight and happiness into many homes which otherwise would be debarred from the pleasure and refining influence of music, as also affording novelty and pleasure to those even, whose circumstances permit them to indulge their taste in a costly organ or piano. The catalogue of music prepared for the Autophone now embraces nearly 1,000 tunes—sacred and instrumental music, popular airs and the operas—and the more fully it is understood and introduced the more popular it must become. Letters patent were first granted Mr. Horton for the Autophone in October, 1877, and again in December, 1878, and he tried to interest capital in the formation of a company for its manufacture, but was then unsuccessful, owing to the fact that special music, differing materially from that used in other automatic musical instruments, was required, and there was a general incredulity as to his ability to construct a machine that would cut it. Having satisfactorily demonstrated this point, however, by the construction of a press, the Autophone Company was formed by F. M. Finch, H. F. Hibbard and H. B. Horton, and in September, 1879, incorporated. A room was secured —half of the second floor—in the west wing of the Ithaca Calendar Clock Company's building and the work of manufacturing the Autophone begun. When placed upon the market its novelty and decided merit won for it immediate popularity, and about 75 Autophones were produced monthly, until in the spring of 1880, when the whole of this floor was taken and the capacity of the factory about doubled. The demand for them steadily increasing, the capacity was again enlarged during the same year, and early in 1881 the entire west wing of this large building was occupied by the company. During 1882 they manufactured 15,000 of the small sized instruments and 3,000 of the other sizes, and as the demand for the larger instruments is greater this year, the aggregate amount of business for 1883, in dollars, will probably equal the large business of 1882, while the prospects for the future are even brighter. Having purchased Horton's patents, a new organization of the company was effected in April, 1883, and the officers now are F. M. Finch, President ; H. A. St. John, Vice President, and H. M. Hibbard, Treasurer. Mr. St. John and Mr. Hibbard have been actively connected with the company since February, 1881, however, and the latter is especially well versed in the business. Four sizes of the Autophone are made, the smallest instrument

(22 notes) selling for $5; the concert style, $12; concert style, with stand, (32 notes) $16, and the cabinet autophone, $35; and the company are also now manufacturing Prof. Cleaves' Patent Study Table, a most convenient and useful article for the student or writer. A working force of 45 people is employed, which number

is nearly doubled in preparation for the holiday trade, and the facilities for producing the Autophone are of the most complete character. The machinery is principally that specially adapted and invented for this business, and includes five presses for cutting music. These presses are wonders of ingenious mechanism, and it might here be mentioned that the Autophone Company are the only manufacturers of automatic musical instruments who cut their own music. When it is considered what an immense amount of skilled labor is required to produce one of these little instruments it is surprising how they can be sold so cheaply. The reeds are as carefully and accurately tuned as those of an organ, while the material is of the very best quality and the workmanship expended on the cases, on every part of the instrument, is fully equal to that expended on an organ. But the result justifies the expenditure of both the time and money, for the popularity of the Autophone is steadily increasing and it is constantly making new friends and patrons where other automatic musical instruments are being consigned to oblivion. The Autophone Company are just beginning to export their products and with the favorable reception the Autophone is meeting in other countries and the still greater demand here at home they have every reason to feel gratified at their past success as well as pleased with the prospects of the future. They have an abundance of capital, the enterprise is conducted by gentlemen of ability and there is every indication that the industry will not only continue to thrive and prosper, but add still more largely to the wealth, prosperity and industrial reputation of Ithaca.

C. A. IVES.

For the convenient purchase of tickets to all points throughout the world, Ithaca is well supplied with ticket offices right in the heart of the village. Notable among these is the office of C. A. Ives, at No. 3 Clinton block. The office was opened by Mr. Ives about six years ago, and through his courtesy and accuracy he has become well-known to the traveling public, and his office is a favorite place for purchasers of railway and steamship tickets. He is the regular city agent for the Lehigh Valley Railroad. Being thoroughly posted on all lines of travel he is enabled to furnish the most complete information to tourists and others, especially concerning the Great West and its railroads. Baggage is checked from the residences of those purchasing tickets from him, and by reason of the accommodations afforded the traveling public, his office is a great convenience, and is thereby worthy the brief notice given.

SHELDON & BLIVEN.

The best equipped and most popularly managed livery establishment in Ithaca is that of Sheldon & Bliven, located at the foot of South Tioga street. The ground upon which the large and attractive appearing stables and office stand is in some respects historic. Here for many years prior to the great flood of 1857 stood a hat manufactory originally conducted by the Tichenors, and later by the well known hat and fur merchant of to-day, William M. Culver. This building and its contents were carried away and destroyed by the terrible deluge of angry waters which swept through this village on that memorable night twenty-six years ago. In 1879 the firm of Sheldon & Bliven was formed. The senior member of the firm, J. P Sheldon, was for several years previous to that date the proprietor of a livery stable in this place, and the other member of the firm, C. M. Bliven, came here in that year from Norwich, Chenango County. The buildings have been much improved since their occupancy by Sheldon & Bliven, and the business has prospered under the management of these gentlemen. Both are known as excellent judges of horse-flesh, and in addition to owning considerable first-class stock for hire, as well as keeping the most stylish and tasty turnouts the village affords, have in their stables, Pathfinder, a splendid animal for breeding purposes. The establishment of this enterprising firm deservedly receives much of the best patronage of the place.

C. S. WIXOM.

The general art and variety store at 38 East State street, of which Clermont S. Wixom is the proprietor, was established December 1st, 1881, by the firm of Wright & Wixom. In the following May Mr. Wixom purchased Mr. Wright's share of the business and has since conducted it alone. The stock has been much increased and improved under Mr. Wixom's individual proprietorship and his store contains a very full and fine assortment of art, variety and fancy goods. A specialty is made of framing pictures and a large and growing patronage in this department of the business is enjoyed at this store. For holiday and anniversary gifts this well-known and popular, cheap store is the leading headquarters in the county. Excellent taste is shown in the selection of goods, much enterprise is exhibited in acquainting the public with interesting facts relating to the business, and further and growing success is due this well conducted store, which fills an important place in the business resources of Ithaca.

WILLIAM FREAR.

"As familiar as household words" throughout Tompkins County, are the name and high standing, in his profession, of William Frear, the oldest established and most prominent photographer of Ithaca and its vicinity. There is scarcely a household in the county where some evidence of his artistic taste and undoubted skill as a photographer will not be found gracing the pages of the family album. The growth of William Frear's business has kept pace with his increasing artistic excellence and merit, and in both respects it can be truthfully said he stands now in the lead, as regards this place and a considerable surrounding territory. A sketch of the leading events in the professional and business growth of Mr. Frear will form an interesting chapter in ITHACA AND ITS RESOURCES. After getting a thorough training in the elements of photography with the firm of Moulton & Larcom, in the adjacent city of Elmira, Mr. Frear removed to Jamestown, Chautauqua County, in 1865, and there in connection with Alvin Phillips, opened a gallery. In March, 1857, he purchased of George Beardsley his share of the business which had been started by Purdy & Beardsley. The new firm of Purdy & Frear occupied the same quarters on the upper floor of the Pumpelly Block, where Mr. Frear's business is now located. In 1873 Mr. Purdy withdrew from the firm to devote himself to portrait painting, and Mr. Frear has since remained sole proprietor of the business, to which he has greatly added in all ways. Hundreds of dollars have been expended in the finest and newest apparatus obtainable, new scenery and backgrounds have been purchased from time to time, and all new processes in the art have been mastered promptly and put into successful operation at this gallery. The "instantaneous" process, the greatest recent improvement in photography is now almost exclusively practiced by Mr. Frear and his remarkable success in the line of accurate children's pictures, so strongly illustrated by the fine prize exhibition of child pictures made at the late county fair, is largely due to his thorough mastery of this method. While Mr. Frear has not infrequently given evidence of much originality and versatility by his excellently made novelties in the line of photographic studies, among which may be mentioned his "palette" pictures, curious "double" pictures, groups of heads, and season sketches, shown at the fair of 1882, still he is best known for the painstaking care, and faithful accuracy with which his pictures in standard styles are invariably made. So well established is the reputation of Mr. Frear for the naturalness and accuracy of his work that for one to say that a photograph is from his studio is as much as to assert that it is in the great majority of instances, a correct and excellently finished picture. A high standing in a community for thoroughness, enterprise and business worth always challenges the admiration of the public. Such a position is held in Ithaca by William Frear, and it is an augury of even larger success in the future than he has yet enjoyed.

REYNOLDS & LANG.

The business of Reynolds & Lang, the Green Street Iron Founders and Machinists, is the oldest continuous manufacturing business in Ithaca to-day. The growth of this establishment, which is probably the largest of its class in the village, is an illustration of the growth and progress of the "Forest City," and forms an interesting chapter of ITHACA AND ITS RESOURCES. Many readers here will remember the old foundry which for years stood on the present site of the handsome Masonic Block on Tioga street. Here in this old building in 1840 the foundry business was established by the firm of McCormick & Coy. The building was small, about 25x35 feet in dimensions, and the manufacture of stoves and a general jobbing and repair business was done. For some reason it changed hands very frequently. McCormick & Coy were succeeded by the Coy Brothers, and they by Stephen H. Coy. Then John H. Coy tried it but gave place in turn to E. G. Coy in 1844. It was while the establishment was run by the Coy Brothers in 1841 that Mr. J. S. Reynolds, of the present firm of Reynolds & Lang entered the foundry to learn his trade of molding. With the growth of Ithaca this property became more valuable and was purchased by B. G. Pelton. He continued the business for some years and in 1861 Mr. Reynolds, who had served his apprenticeship in the foundry and become a skilled workman, leased it. In 1865 he formed a co-partnership with Mr. J. B. Lang, a practical machinist of large experience, and the business was successfully continued there by them until 1870, when, it being desirable to enlarge, they purchased the site on Green street, near Tioga, now occupied by them and erecting buildings removed from the old shops, upon the site of which the large brick Masonic Block was soon built. Under the management of Reynolds & Lang, the business had been steadily increasing, the manufacture of stoves had been abandoned a long time and the production of mill machinery, building iron and store fronts was the specialty. In 1875 they began building steam engines and boilers, which has since been the leading specialty and they now manufacture portable and stationary engines and boilers, mill gearing, agricultural implements, &c. The buildings were considerably enlarged in 1877, and the old machinery being replaced by new, the equipment is now equal to all demands, and forms a valuable plant. The main building is a three story frame structure, fronting 63 feet on Green street and 40 feet deep. The first floor is occupied by the machine shop and office and the second and third floors by the wood working and finishing departments. In the rear are the foundry, 40x50 feet in dimensions and the boiler shop, 50x30 feet. A force of 30 men is employed and a large number of engines are built annually, besides a large amount of mill gearing and other work. Their portable threshing and farm engine is considered the best engine for the purpose manufactured, by the farmers in this State, it being noted for economy in the amount of fuel required for the power furnished. All their products, however, are noted for quality and workmanship, as would naturally be expected from a firm that were practical workmen and iron founders and machinists in reality and not simply in name. Having so far kept pace with the progress made by Ithaca it is not likely the growth of the establishment will stop now, and it may be with confidence expected that Reynolds & Lang will advance still farther and add still more largely to the prosperity of this place.

J. H. HORTON.

In 1876 the Lehigh Valley Coal Company established an agency in this place, putting its important interests here into the hands of Col. J. H. Horton, who had for some years previously been in the employ of the Anthracite Coal Company, as superintendent of the mines in Sullivan County, Pennsylvania. Col. Horton has proved a very efficient and popular representative of the Lehigh Valley Coal Company, and has had not a little to do with the very large increase in business at this point which the company has obtained in the last six years. Figures, far better than adjectives, convey a correct idea of the growth of a business, as well as its present status. In 1877 the Lehigh Valley Company shipped by water from this point 40,000 tons of coal. During the present season the amount shipped by water will reach 165,000 tons. The facilities for handling coal have been largely increased, a new dock being now in process of construction, and next year an additional dock will be built. Where formerly not more than 25,000 tons of coal could be stocked, now 100,000 tons can be stocked and still more room is needed. On the docks sixty laborers are employed and besides a foreman and four clerks. There is sold from the retail department annually 15,000 tons of anthracite coal and 11,000 tons of bituminous coal. The Ithaca Agency is the headquarters for the Valley Company's Western trade, and the through shipments over the G. I. & S. railroad are very large. During the current year closing Nov. 30th the amount of hard coal passing this point will reach nearly 500,000 tons, and to this must be added 60,000 tons of soft coal. The property of the Lehigh Valley Coal Company at this point amounts to upwards of $100,000 in value and this is to be largely increased in the future. The large enrerprise of which Col J. H. Horton is the very capable manager, adds much to the commercial importance of Ithaca.

ANDRUS & CHURCH.

Probably few of the readers are aware of the fact that at one time Ithaca was widely known as a publishing centre. But such is a fact, and many years ago the house now bearing the name of Andrus & Church was engaged in publishing educational and other books which found a wide market, among their customers being one of the largest publishing houses now engaged in business in New York City. But what will seem still more notable is that not only were the books printed and bound by this publishing house, but that the paper upon which they were printed was also manufactured by them, and branch houses were established in Elmira, Hornellsville and other cities throughout the country for the sale of their publications and those of other publishers, with whom they exchanged their books. That day has passed, that place of business has been abandoned, and many relics of that time were destroyed when the old fashioned three-story building which stood on the present site of the handsome Andrus & Church block at No. 51 East State street, and in which for so many years that business was conducted, was burned in April of 1871. That old landmark is gone, an imposing brick structure stands in its place, the character of the business has somewhat changed, and the son of the leading spirit of the old house is at the head of the house now conducting it. William Andrus was born at Harwinton, Conn., November 18, 1800. At the age of ten years he lost his father by death and was thrown upon his own resources. He was fortunate, however, in falling into the hands of an intelligent and religious New England farmer who instilled into the boy's mind those lessons of integrity, uprightness and economy which can hardly be else than productive of good. At the age of sixteen he went to New York and entered into the employ of a printer named Paul, with whom he remained until 1823. Here again he was fortunate in his associations and the principles taught him by the former became more deeply fixed in his mind. While traveling as an auctioneer for his elder brother Silas, a bookseller in Hartford, Conn., in 1824, he visited Ithaca. His prompt attention to business, gentlemanly politeness, retiring demeanor and high-toned integrity impressed all with whom he came in contact, but more especially Mr. Ebenezer Mack, then engaged in the book trade and the publication of the *Journal*. After he left Ithaca, Mr. Mack wrote him and made proposals of partnership. The proposition was accepted by Mr. Andrus and in the fall of 1824 he removed to Ithaca, and the firm of Mack & Andrus was formed. The name of the firm and the character of the business changed several times. In 1835 or 1836 it became Mack, Andrus & Woodruff; in 1842, Andrus, Woodruff & Gauntlett; then Andrus, Gauntlett & Co., and in 1859, Andrus, McChain & Co. An exceedingly large business was built up, and it was during this period—the exact date is not within reach—that the large publishing business of which mention is made in the opening of this sketch was conducted. William Andrus acquired a competence and died an honored and lamented citizen, December 20, 1869. His son, William Andrus, took his place in the firm, which continued as Andrus, McChain & Co., until 1869, when the present firm of Andrus & Church was formed by William Andrus and W. A. Church. The business of Andrus & Church, the successors of this old house, is now that of dealers in books and stationery and printers and binders. They occupy the first **floor of their** large block, 25x80 feet in dimensions, as a salesroom for books, stationery, wall paper, etc., carrying a large stock and fine assortment of everything in this line, especially publications in demand by students at the University. In the rear of this building is a three-story brick structure occupied by the printing office and bindery. There are five presses in operation and a fully equipped bindery and printing office in the building. From 10 to 12 people are employed by them, and besides the regular book and pamphlet work, blank book manufacturing and general job printing done they also print the University publications, the Cornell *Review* (monthly), *Era* (weekly) and *Sun* (daily). They do a large business and rank among the foremost of Ithaca's business houses.

THE ITHACA GLASS WORKS.

The glass industry is becoming of considerable prominence in Ithaca, and there is certainly no other that could be more welcome. The new Ithaca Glass Works give employment to 150 workmen, and pay out $9,000 in wages every month. This simple statement is sufficient to show its value to the community, and the starting up anew of the works is consequently hailed with much satisfaction. Originally established in 1874, the works changed owners in 1876, and were successfully conducted until April of 1882, when they were destroyed by fire. A new company was subsequently organized, however, and the works were re-built, being completed during the past summer (1883,) and are now in full operation. This is one of the largest and best arranged glass works in the country, and the visitor will be at once impressed by the size of the immense buildings, especially of the main furnace building, which is 100x205 feet in dimensions. To the architect or builder, the supporting of such a large roof without pillars forms an interesting study. This building contains two eight-pot furnaces. An annex furnace building, with a third eight-pot furnace, is now building, and will be 75x100 feet in dimensions. The flattening and annealing building is 150x90 feet, while the building occupied by the cutting and packing departments is 28x90 feet. The building in which are the engine room, mill for grinding the crucible material and the box shop is 30x120 feet. The crucible building, where the melting pots are made, is a two-story frame structure, 30x100 feet, and the batch house is 28x50 feet. No concern in this country possesses better facilities, either for manufacturing glass or for the receipt of material and shipment of product. The works are located on Third street, between Franklin and Railroad, within a couple hundred feet of the canal, and lie between the Geneva, Ithaca and Sayre, and Delaware, Lackawana and Western Railroads, with sidings from both roads running directly into their yards. A trestle capable of receiving 15 coal cars runs alongside the main furnace building and permits the dumping of coal just where it is most convenient, while the yard track permits 20 freight cars to stand in the yard at one time for loading or unloading. Sixty cars are received and put out from the works every week. About 900 tons of coal, 150 cords of wood, 65 tons of soda-ash, and 250 tons of sand (the latter coming from Oneida Lake by canal,) are consumed in the production of the monthly output of 9,000 boxes of glass. Both single and double thick Patent White Crystal Sheet Glass is produced, the works being built according to the most improv-

ed plans for the economical production of a superior quality of glass. This being the commencement of the first season of the works, it is a source of much gratification to the stockholders in the concern, that their new and expensive plant is working so satisfactorily, the glass being of a uniformly fine quality. The works were built under the direction of Mr. Richard Heagany, the superintendent, who has been connected with them since 1876. And he may well feel a pardonable pride in the result of his labors. The Ithaca Glass Works are owned by a stock company, of which the officers are Messrs. C. F. Blood, President; D. F. Williams, Vice-President; William N. Noble, Treasurer; Bradford Almy, Secretary; and Richard Heagany, Superintendent. These gentlemen are all well and favorably known as being among the leading citizens of Ithaca, and they certainly could confer no greater benefit upon the "Forest City" than they have in building these works, and re-establishing an industry of so much value to the place. It is to be hoped that the auspicious opening of the works under this new management will only prove to be the forerunner of greater success to come, and when again the Resources of Ithaca are thus reviewed, the Ithaca Glass Works will be found to have fulfilled not only the expectations of the promoters of the enterprise, but have served, through its success, to attract other industries to this beautiful village, which offers so many advantages to manufacturing enterprises of every description.

E. S. ESTY & SONS.

In the year 1821 there were in existence two establishments devoted to the business of tanning in what was then the hamlet of Ithaca. One was situated upon the grounds now occupied by the beautiful residences of Calvin D. Stowell and Arthur B. Brooks on North Aurora street, and was owned by Daniel Bates, whose name is closely identified with the early history of this place. The other tannery stood upon the lot at the southeast corner of Aurora and Buffalo streets and was owned by Comfort Butler, by whom the house now occupied by Alexander King was built in 1817. The late Joseph Esty, who had for sometime previous been employed as foreman of the tannery of the Messrs. Patty, of Auburn, learning that the Butler tannery could be rented, gathered the small earnings accruing from the salary of $300 a year, which was large, however, for those times, and borrowing the sum of $1000 beside, came to Ithaca and commenced business on his own account. From this humble beginning has grown in due time the large and flourishing enterprise now conducted by Edward S. Esty, eldest son of Joseph Esty, and Albert H., and Clarence H., sons of E. S. Esty. When Joseph Esty first established himself here there were in Tompkins County some twenty-four or twenty-five tanneries, but the only hides used were those of the domestic animals of the county, unless perchance a trip to Albany was made by some enterprising farmer who had wheat to sell, when a small quantity of Spanish hides, as any foreign hides were then called, were brought back as the return load. Within a few years thereafter Mr. Esty purchased of Simeon DeWitt the premises at the corner of Tioga and Green streets, now occupied by the planing mill of George Small, and removed his business to that site. In the great fire of 1871 the buildings were entirely destroyed, and the business which was under full headway at the time received a temporary check. In a short time, however, the works were rebuilt on a much larger scale on their present site in the southwestern part of the village. The present Ithaca tannery possesses all of the improvements known to the trade, including the novelty of a circular railroad. The capacity of the works is 50,000 sides of sole leather each year. The firm of E. S. Esty & Sons also owns two other tanneries of the same capacity, which are located at Candor and Catatonk in Tioga County. The leather from all of these tanneries bears the trade mark "Humboldt," and is mainly sold in Boston, Mass. Long experience in the business, however, has made them familiar with the markets of the world and they avail themselves of this knowledge in the purchase of hides as well as the sale of the products of their factories. It is a curious fact that in these extensive tanneries are to be found the skins of animals from nearly every part of the globe (except Tewksbury.) The question is sometimes asked "why not use the hides of our own domestic cattle, or those of Europe?" The answer is that these animals are too well fed, and the improvement in stock of late years has caused the deposition of a large amount of the fatty elements in the hides. This together with the shelter of our domestic animals in sheds and barns in the winter, renders their hides thin and tender and adapted only for harness and "upper" leather purposes. There is no product of this place or immediate vicinity, which enters into the manufactures of these tanneries, except labor. The bark comes largely from the forests of Pennsylvania, and Southern New York, and as has been stated the hide supply is drawn from all parts of the world. As showing how greatly the tannery interests represented by E. S. Esty and Sons exceed in dimensions those of the early days of this vicinity, it may be stated that their works located on the Cayuga inlet in Ithaca, annually produce more leather than the whole twenty-five tanneries of Tompkins County of fifty years ago could by the processes then known to the trade have produced in three years. While for many years Edward S. Esty has given to the business established by his father, and so largely developed by himself and sons, the greater share of his energy and thoughtful attention, he has still found opportunity, and great satisfaction as well, in matters pertaining to the general well being of the trade in which he has so greatly succeeded, to his native village, among whose honored and highly respected citizens he is a leader, and in the State, to whose highest legislative councils he has lately been called by an election to the Senate from this, the 26th district. As a citizen of Ithaca he has held, and still occupies, many important positions. He was the first chief engineer of the fire department in its present form, and framed the laws by which it is governed. He was one of the incorporators of the First National Bank, and now is vice president of this flourishing financial concern. He was trustee and treasurer of the old academy, and has been for years a trustee of the Cornell Library, and President of the Board of Education since the establishment of the present graded school system. The recent adoption of Mr. Esty's suggestion in relation to the building of a new high school edifice at a cost of $50,000 is a timely illustration of his liberal and progressive ideas in connection with educational affairs. Mr. Esty will not enter the Senate an entire stranger to the legislative halls, as in 1858 he represented Tompkins County in the Assembly. For years he had taken no active part in politics, and his nomination for the senatorship from this district came all unsought and unexpectedly. His election was a fitting testimonial of the high regard in which the gentleman is held, and his career in the Senate will amply prove the wisdom of his selection to fill this important position, as it will give better scope than ever for the exercise of his ripened experience, and sound practical judgment.

THE ITHACA SIGN WORKS.

Within the last decade advertising in all its different forms has increased very largely, and especially is this noticeable in driving through the country. On nearly every fence or barn or tree is tacked a board sign calling attention to this or to that remedy, or the different stores in the towns near by. Very many of these signs are made in Ithaca, and their manufacture forms quite an industry. The third floor of Small's planing mill building, at the corner of Green and Tioga streets, is occupied by the Ithaca Sign Works, of which Stanford & Co. are the proprietors. Here a number of men, boys and girls are employed in painting, printing and finishing these sign boards and other advertising novelties, which are shipped to every State and Territory in the Union. Besides the rooms in this building, a room in another building is occupied for the painting of the large picture signs on gum cloth, in which a considerable business is done, and three or four people are also employed outside in finishing up some of the work. Three men are employed in traveling throughout the country and soliciting orders for the products of the establishment, which embrace board, tin and cloth advertising signs, advertising novelties, such as yard sticks, match safes, knife sharpeners and picture signs of every description, both humorous and otherwise, which are all made to order. The gentlemen composing the firm of Stanford and Company are practical men, and have evidently reduced the business to a system. The best advertisers in the country are numbered among their patrons, and the concern is probably the largest of its kind in the country.

ITHACA TELEPHONE SERVICE.

It is not within the province of this sketch to follow in detail the gradual development of the telephone system in Ithaca. It must suffice concerning the earlier history of the service to note that the early experiments of Prof. W. A. Anthony, of the University, resulted in due time in the formation of a company for the practical conduct and extension of the system. Among the gentlemen most prominently associated with Prof. Anthony in this enterprise was Captain W. O. Wyckoff. The business was put successfully into operation under the direction of these gentlemen and remained under their management until January 1st, of the present year, when it was purchased by the New York & Pennsylvania Telephone & Telegraph Company. By this change in ownership the telephone service of this place has during the year been relieved of its purely local and somewhat amateurish aspect and has become an important link in the great system now extending through seventeen counties of this State and Pennsylvania, which has been developed through the capital and enterprise of this company. The territory at present occupied by the New York & Pennsylvania Telephone & Telegraph Co. embraces the entire northern tier of counties of Pennsylvania, save Wayne, at the extreme eaastern side of the State, and the whole southern tier of

New York, with two of the counties of the second tier. This district contains now more than 4,200 miles of telephone wire, and 3,700 complete sets of instruments, and telephone facilities are thus afforded to a population of 900,000 people. The value of the system is constantly being increased by the extension of direct lines to important points and the adoption of all the best improvements in the art as they become known. With the change of ownership of the telephone service in Ithaca have come other important modifications and improvements. The exchange has been removed from its lofty location in the Rumsey Block to a more eligible site in the Morrison Block; in place of the old time and unsatisfactory switch board the handsome and admirable Williams improved switch board has been put into the exchange; the wires have been taken from the house-tops and placed upon fine poles; and the conduct of the business here has been placed in the hands of a practical electrician and telephone manager, and courteous gentleman, in the person of Mr. James W. Gillespie, formerly of Scranton, Pa. Mr. Gillespie's assumption of the management of the telephone service in Ithaca dated October 1st. Already the beneficial effects upon the service resulting from the efforts of a capable, experienced manager are apparent. New confidence has been inspired in the public, not a few new subscribers have been secured, and in many ways the value of the system has been much augmented. In the whole territory occupied by the New York & Pennsylvania Telephone & Telegraph Company this village is the only one in which hand telephones are still in use. By January 1st, 1884, they will have entirely disappeared from use here as well. This fact, together with the improvement in the conduct of the exchange, in the matter of prompt response to calls, and in all other possible ways, will fully make up in the added efficiency of the service the increased yearly rental which is now required. In this connection it may be said that in no other place in the United States of equal size are the same facilities, namely, a full set of instruments and communication by a direct line, provided as cheaply as in Ithaca. There are now 148 subscribers to the telephone system here, and from 400 to 600 calls are responded to daily at the exchange. It may be confidently predicted that in the hands of so efficient and wide awake a gentleman as Manager Gillespie the interests of his employers will be well cared for, and the rights and conveniences of the public will be equally and thoroughly observed.

WILLIAM M. CULVER.

The business career of this long established and successful merchant began in Massilon, Ohio, in 1841, where at the age of 21 he entered upon the manufacturing and sale of hats and the handling of furs. Eight years later he returned to Ithaca, and opened a store at the corner of Cayuga and State streets, in the building now occupied by Crozier & Feeley. He next removed to a store in the Stannard Block, which occupied the site of the present store of R. A. Heggie. Then his business was transferred two years later to the Krum building at the corner of State and Tioga streets. His next move was to purchase the stock in the store of J. S. Tichenor, which was then in the building on East State street, now occupied by S. Harrison. At the same time Mr. Culver bought Tichenor's hat manufactory which then stood on the bank of Six Mile Creek, where Sheldon &

Bliven's livery stable is now situated. This building and its contents were carried away by the great flood of 1857. The business of manufacturing hats was never resumed after this disaster. Giving his entire attention to the retail sale of hats and fur goods, thereafter, Mr. Culver succeeded in building up a good trade and in time was able to repair the damage done by the flood. About 1865 he purchased the store building at 64 East State street, which he took possession of a few months later and has occupied up to the present time. Mr. Culver is one of the reliable, conservative business men of Ithaca. His success has been achieved by unremitting industry, prudence and honorable dealing, through a long term of years.

SHEPHERD & DOYLE.

In the early history of any community its stores are few and they contain an assortment of goods of all kinds so that the various wants of all may be supplied at one place. With the growth and development of the village, the era of "country stores" passes away, and as the place takes on more and more the character of a city, specialty stores are established in which the sale of a certain limited line of goods is conducted. During the last few years several such stores have been established here. Among them is the ladies' and gentlemen's furnishing goods business of Shepherd & Doyle occupying a handsome store at 58 East State street. This partnership was formed in the spring of 1880 and a store was taken at 9 North Tioga street. A good trade was soon built up in this place, but after a time the firm became desirous of securing a location on the main street. The store at 58 East State street became vacant, and after it had been modernized with a fine plate glass front, and other improvements, was taken possession of by this thriving young firm in the spring of 1882. The stock was increased and improved and the business took a new impetus. It has prospered well since, the store having become the recognized headquarters for gentlemen's furnishing goods in great variety of cost and make, as well as for many articles of feminine wear, a specialty being made of corsets. The display of this class of goods made by the firm at the late fair of the County Agricultural Society attracted much attention on account of its extent and the large variety of makes shown.

POST, SHARP & CO.

With our more rapid strides in the march of progress comes an increasing demand for novelty. This demand for novelty is not confined to any one particular branch of business, but extends into every line of industry. A nation less blessed in resources could not possibly fill this demand, but what is beyond the possibilities of American ingenuity is as yet unlearned. Especially in the way of wheeled vehicles for both business and pleasure driving, has this demand for novelty been felt within the last year or two, and manufacturers have been compelled to exercise their ingenuity to the utmost to keep pace with the demand. The manufactory of four wheeled vehicles having been reduced to such a system that the limits of perfection and accuracy have been almost reached, with the restlessness and unsatisfiableness peculiar to the American people comes that unceasing demand for something new, and the attention of manufacturers has consequently been turned to two-wheelers as being possibly the only field that

that promises to satisfy, for the present, this craving for novelty. But here comes a point upon which most of them have been impaled. The English village cart has been a favorite vehicle with fashionable people in England for many years, no English establishment being complete without it, and the village cart naturally found its way to this country, as "society" here must have that which is pronounced fashionable there. But the English village cart is far from being a pleasant vehicle in which to ride, the swinging, jolting motion given to it by the horse being, in fact, decidedly disagreeable, while unless a horse of just the the proper size is hitched to it, the cart is either tipped up behind and down in front, or *vice versa*, in either case the position of the occupant being an uncomfortable one, and the drive proving anything but pleasurable. Like in the wearing of high-heeled and tight fitting shoes, however, the devotees of fashion would have them. and as the village cart is principally designed for ladies and children, the road cart, in all its various shapes was constructed to supply the wants of gentlemen. But this same trouble was experienced with all "two-wheelers," village or road carts, and the swinging, jolting motion given to them by the horse, and the difficulty of fitting them to large and small horses, was the point upon which manufacturers were impaled as it were—the objection which they were unable to satisfactorily overcome, while their road carts,also, presented too much the appearance of a sulky. And while a limited number of village and road carts were produced, to meet the demands of the extremists of fashion, it was quickly discovered by manufacturers that unless they could successfully obviate these difficulties, two-wheelers, although they might become fashionable, would never attain popularity and come into general use. Manufacturers in all parts of the country have attempted the solution of this problem, as this demand for novelty became more painfully apparent, but the only really successful solvers as yet are the Ithaca firm of Post, Sharp & Co., and they have so fully overcome these objections and covered every possible and feasible point of improvement with letters patent, that it is doubtful whether any of the manufacturers will continue their attempts, as the solution can hardly be found without infringing on their patents. In the Ithaca Road and Village Carts, that swinging, jolting motion, so commonly experienced in two-wheelers, is entirely overcome, while the greatest point of improvement is probably in the adjustable shafts, whereby a road or village cart can in five minutes time, without necessitating any change in harness, be abjusted to fit the largest horse or smallest pony, so that the body of the cart sets perfectly level. No road or village cart is perfect unless it can be so adjusted and changed at will, and it it is obvious that the only proper place where such change can be made is in the shafts. The device used in the Ithaca Road and Village Cart consists of a thill provided intermediately of its length with a vertically deflecting joint and a clamping device for retaining said joint in its requisite angle. It is simple, yet strong and durable. The body is set on a platform spring, made expressly for these carts, and hung on these finely adjusted springs and perfectly balanced, its motion is as easy as that of the finest riding four-wheeled vehicles. The road carts are built with White Chapel, Corning and Piano bodies, and do not in the least present the appearance of a sulky, or possess the disagreeable features and peculiarities of that vehicle; but are a

light, stylish, easy riding, two-wheeled vehicle of good proportions, strong, well made and finely finished. The favor with which the Ithaca Road and Village Carts have been received is unprecedented, and in overcoming the difficulties which formerly prevented two-wheelers coming into general use, Post, Sharp & Co. have evidently paved their way for a brilliant and successful career. The history of this concern is a brief one, for it has only been in existence a short time. On the 3d day of January, 1882, the copartnership of Post & Sharp was formed for the purpose of manufacturing the Ithaca Plow Sulky. The building standing on the old Fair Grounds, near the Ithaca Calendar Clock Company's works, was secured, and the work of building plow sulkies begun with a force of eight workmen. The plow sulkies possess many features of superiority over those of other patents, and their manufacture was continued throughout the year with much success. But having obtained patents for the features which make the coming into general use of road and village carts not only possible, but more than probable, in the latter part of the year (December) they commenced making preparations for building the light and tasty two-wheelers which have since met with such great success. On the 5th day of January, 1883, Mr. N. S Johnson became a member of this copartnership, the title of the firm was changed to Post, Sharp & Co., and the work of building road and village carts and skeleton wagons, the peculiar features of which are all covered by letters patent, was begun. The working force was increased to thirty employes, a systematic method of building the vehicles was introduced, and in a month a number were handsomely finished and placed upon the market. Success was instantaneous, the Ithaca Road and Village Carts jumped into popularity immediately and the demand was greater than the supply. And this demand has not only continued throughout the year, but gives promise of a steady and still greater increase as the vehicles are more fully introduced and their merits become understood. Several styles of the Ithaca Road Cart, with or without tops to suit the needs and tastes of all, are manufactured, which have the same room, the same style of bodies, the same ease and comfort that there is in the finest riding side-bar or end-spring buggy. Making a specialty of the two wheelers they have perfected, and their factory being especially equipped for this branch of business, Post, Sharp & Co. have every advantage over their competitors and will undoubtedly be the leaders in this industry. The main building of their factory is 50x100 feet in dimensions, four floors, and the blacksmith shop is 30x50 feet. Both buildings are thoroughly equipped with improved labor-saving iron and wood-working machinery, driven by an engine of 35 horse power. Adjoining the works is the lumber yard, with sheds for storage, and here is a 52-inch circular saw for sawing out the heavy lumber. Of the main building are saws, planers, &c., for working out the many pieces entering into the construction of these vehicles, and in the rear of this department is the packing and shipping room. The second floor occupied by the wood-finishing, gear and body painting (finishing), and upholstering departments. The third floor is devoted to the storage of bodies for hardening and the fourth floor is occupied by the rough painting and rubbing-in departments. An excellent hoisting apparatus makes this arrangement of the building as convenient as could be desired. The blacksmith shop is equipped with drop hammers, die presses, &c., and the most skilled workers in iron, wood and painting are employed. With the aid of the machinery and the systematic method adopted, the vehicles are rapidly produced and finished in the most highly satisfactory manner. The production for this their first year will be about 700 Road and Village Carts and Skeleton Wagons, with the prospects favorable for doubling this production next year. Individually, the members of the firm are gentlemen peculiarly well fitted for making the business a success. Mr. C. C. Post is a capitalist, formerly of Geneva, and well known as a young gentleman of enterprise, shrewdness and ability. Mr. D. P. Sharp is a practical man understanding the detail of manufacturing, and in superintending the mechanical department gives assurance of good workmanship. Mr. N. S. Johnson, by reason of his large experience in the wagon business in the east and west, is one whose ability is recognized by the trade, and will do much towards making the firm's popularity as great as the merit of their products deserve. They are certainly starting under the most auspicious circumstances, and as the policy of using only the best material and employing best workmen in the production of their vehicles is being carrried out almost to the extreme, there can be no doubt as to their future and still greater success. The industry is one that can be developed into a large labor employing concern of great value to Ithaca, and these gentlemen are undoubtedly on the right way to accomplish that result.

GEORGE GRIFFIN.

Undoubtedly the leading merchant tailor of Ithaca is George Griffin, whose fine store situated in the Masonic Block, North Tioga street, is a credit to the place. The business of which Mr. Griffin is the enterprising and successful proprietor was founded many years ago by General Charles F. Blood. In 1873 the business was removed from a small store on East State street to its present fine quarters. Mr. Griffin's connection with the establishment began shortly prior to that time. In 1882 Gen. Blood withdrew from the business, Mr. Griffin purchasing the stock and good will. The excellent patronage formerly enjoyed by this fine store has been fully maintained under Mr Griffin's direction. A very large and fine stock of cloths is carried, first-class cutters and tailors are employed, and the work of the establishment will compare favorably with the best work of metropolitan tailors.

ENZ & MILLER.

Among the important commercial enterprises of Ithaca, which have had their rise and growth during the present decade, one of the leading is the wholesale paper and stationery business of Messrs. Enz & Miller, located in the Titus Block. The members of this firm for a considerable time were in the employ of the late firm of Andrus & McChain. In June, 1878, with a moderate capital, but plenty of business experience, a wide commercial acquaintance, and a large amount of push and business acumen, the members of this firm, viz.: Frank J. Enz and Thomas G. Miller, opened a store at No. 20 North Aurora street. They met with success from the beginning and rapidly increased their lines, as their volume of trade increased. In the spring of 1880, finding their store in Aurora street too contracted, they removed to their present large and conveniently located store in the Titus Block. Success has continued to attend the steps of this enterprising firm, their business having tripled since their removal to their State street quarters. The stock carried is very large and complete in all respects, and the reputation of the firm for strict integrity and reliability is widely known throughout this section of the state. The rapid growth of their business is the natural result of the fitness for the work of its proprietors, the demand which existed here for such an establishment and the intelligent manner in which it has been conducted from the outset. Further and larger commercial prosperity is plainly before this admirably equipped business house.

ACKLEY'S NEWS ROOM.

This business was established in 1850 by Julius Ackley, one of the best known earlier residents of the place. This news room was the first business of the kind established in Ithaca and was originally in the old post office building which stood on the site of the Vant Block on North Tioga street. At the death of the original proprietor the business passed into the hands of his daughter, Miss Cornelia Ackley, and has continued in her hands to the present time. When the post office was removed in 1882 from the Library Building to its present location on State street, a fine store three doors east of the post office was leased by Miss Ackley, and her business was transferred from the small frame building adjoining the County Clerk's office to its present commodious quarters, No. 19 East State street. A fine line of stationery and fancy goods has been added to the former stock. A full line of stereoscopic views of Cornell University, and of the romantic scenery of Ithaca and vicinity is kept constantly by Miss Ackley, and orders by mail are promptly supplied in all cases. The business is in all respects the leading one of its kind in this vicinity.

THE BOSTON VARIETY STORE.

This successful and growing business was removed from the neighboring city of Binghamton in April, 1882. At that time it was in the hands of M. H. & E. Wolff. Several months later the business passed into the hands of Jacob Rothschild, the courteous and enterprising manager for the Messrs. Wolff. Under the proprietorship of Mr. Rothschild the stock has been largely increased, and the volume of trade has grown continuously. The business occupies the basement and ground floor of the Smith block, at the northwest corner of State and Aurora streets. The fine store is a perfect museum in its endless variety of articles for personal and house service and ornamentation. The stock includes a large line of ladies' and gentlemen's furnishing goods, china, crockery, glass, tin and wooden ware, bird cages, pictures, toys, lamps, cutlery, and a host of novelties of all kinds. This store justly ranks as one of the most interesting and successful newer ventures of the place.

MRS. L. A. BURRITT.

In 1867 Mrs. L. A. Burritt opened at 24 East State street what was for several years known as the "Thread and Needle store". The business conducted at the outset was, as may be imagined, of a small and modest character, but its proprietor possessed in large measure, as the sequel has shown, the requisites of business success, namely, shrewdness, industry and enterprise In 1870 trade had sufficiently increased to warrant the renting of a larger and better store, and the place of business at 30 E. State street, now occupied, was taken possession of. The stock in trade was increased by the addition of millinery, ladies' and childrens' wear, fancy goods, and embroidery, and business continued to grow each year until Mrs. Burritt's establishment has come to be one of the most richly stocked and prosperous millinery and fancy goods houses of this vicinity. She has only recently returned from a business and pleasure trip to Europe, where considerable purchases of fine French hats and fancy goods were made in Paris. Other additions to her fine stock were purchased in New York, and Mrs. Burritt is once more to be found in her handsome store, refreshed by travel, and with much larger and better facilities for supplying the varied wants of the feminine public than ever before.

A RECORD OF FIFTY YEARS.

In 1832 an office for the practice of dentistry was opened on Seneca street in this village by two gentlemen under the associated style of Miles & Dunning. This firm enjoyed a respectable patronage for that time, and put into practice no little skill and as much knowledge of the art as was available at that comparatively early period in the history of modern dentistry. In course of time the firm became Miles & Bartlett, and an office was opened in the Clinton Block. At a later date, or to speak more definitely, in January, 1858, the firm of Bartlett & Hoysradt was formed and the office in the Clinton Block was continued. Much time was passed in the metropolis, alternately, by each member of the firm, as each was desirous of securing all the information obtainable regarding the newer and advanced methods of practice. In 1859 Dr. G. W. Hoysradt succeeded to the full control of the business, and entered upon a prosperous career which has gone steadily on to the present time. The quarters in the Clinton Block were retained until 1871, when the elegant residence and offices, now occupied by Dr. Hoysradt, having been completed, were taken possession of by him. The early thorough training and metropolitan experience of Dr. Hoysradt, added to rare natural qualifications, soon gave him a richly deserved reputation as an exceedingly skillful operator. With increasing patronage and responsibilities came no neglect in the acquirement of newer ideas, methods and appliances in dentistry and dental surgery. All that was desirable in the advancing stages of the profession was seized upon and embodied in the Doctor's practice, and his attractive parlors have in consequence been visited, and his skilled services put into requisition, by not only our own citizens of the highest classes, but by hundreds from surrounding cities and towns, and adjoining States as well. All branches of the profession are carried on by Dr. Hoysradt and his accomplished assistant Dr. Wm. Hughes, but in the department of filling Dr. Hoysradt has now a reputation for skill and delicacy of manipulation not surpassed, if indeed it is equaled, by that of any dental surgeon in this section of the State. All other operations upon the natural teeth, and the introduction of false teeth by the latest improved methods, are practiced at this establishment. It is with pleasure that the large success of Dr. Hoysradt in his chosen profession has been dwelt upon. His establishment is a model of unobtrusive elegance in all its appointments, a decided ornament and credit to this lovely village, and himself without a superior in the attributes of courteous gentlemanliness and perfect adaptedness to the profession which he has graced for a quarter of a century.

FINCH & APGAR.

The book and stationery business located in the fine brick building at the northwest corner of State and Tioga streets, conducted by Messrs. D. F. Finch and G. W. Apgar, was established more than fifty years ago by the late D. D. Spencer. The business was formerly located in a building occupying a site directly west of the Ithaca Hotel. At the death of the founder, his son, Spence Spencer, succeeded to the business. In 1860 it was purchased by Geo. W. Apgar, who in turn sold to Dudley F. Finch. Mr. Finch later became associated with J. B. Taylor, and by these gentlemen the business was transferred to its present location. The building originally occupied having been destroyed by fire, the handsome block now standing on this site was erected in 1868 and has since continuously been occupied as a book store. Mr. Apgar who had been absent in Cortland and New York returned to Ithaca in 1873 and opened a book store in the Hotel Block. A few months later a second copartnership was formed by Messrs. Finch and Apgar, and the business for nine years has gone on very prosperously under their joint ownership. A large and fine stock of books, University and school text books, mathematical instruments, gold pens, stationery, and wall paper is carried, and an excellent and growing patronage is enjoyed. A very complete book-bindery is conducted in connection with the store, and blank books and writing pads are also manufactured in considerable quantities, two stories of the south store of the new Cornell-Smith Block on South Tioga street being occupied for these purposes. A fair demand for this class of goods has already been established in several of the larger commercial centres of the country, and the prospects are good for the building up of an important trade in this department.

ANDREWS & ALDRICH.

The firm whose name heads this article, though only recently formed, is in point of the extent of business transacted under its management, entitled to rank among the leading mercantile houses of Ithaca. The firm was organized in 1881 and the stock of the large business which had been for a number of years successfully conducted by D. B. Stewart in the building now occupied by Andrews & Aldrich, was purchased. Both members of the firm brought into the business a considerable amount of experience and a large stock of push, pluck and enterprise. I. C. Andrews, the senior member, had been in the employ of D. B. Stewart for five years, and prior to that time, for four years had been in charge of the crockery and grocery department of the large store of H. L. Wilgus and his immediate successors. Fred E. Aldrich began business on his own account seven years ago in McLean, where with C. R. Williams he operated a small store for the sale of general merchandise, under the style of C. R. Williams & Co. Mr. Williams' share in the business was afterwards sold to E. E. Ellis, of Etna, and the business was removed to that village. The firm of Ellis & Aldrich had a prosperous career for two years when Mr. Aldrich sold out his share to his partner, and removed to Ithaca to enter the partnership with I. C. Andrews. The large business which these young but pushing merchants succeeded to, has been constantly increased, and never was more prosperous than at present. During the past year the sales have been greater than in any previous year in the history of the business done in that store. The trade of the firm extends into many surrounding counties of this State, and into Pennsylvania also. They are manufacturers of several cheap brands of cigars, and of confectionery of excellent quality and to a considerable extent. Their business as wholesale dealers in fruit is the most extensive in the place, and in addition they operate an excellent bakery and retail groceries and provisions in large quantities. The business gives employment to about fifteen men and the firm's sales for the year will aggregate $100,000. This is a splendid showing for this young, and go-ahead firm, and forms a good illustration of the old truism that "pluck makes luck."

GEORGE RANKIN & SON.

From a humble start made many years ago, when the highest demand in the trade of this locality was for nothing richer than white china ornamented with plain gold bands, the business of George Rankin & Son, at 42 East State street, has steadily grown and the character of the trade changed and improved, until now the demand is large for the best imported china and cut glass ware, fine bronzes, and the most elaborate wares known to the trade generally. A full supply of goods of this nature is kept constantly on hand by them, or procured from time to time to meet the growing higher taste of the public. But before dwelling more in detail upon the resources of this well known and very successful firm a short sketch of its origin and growth will not be uninteresting. George Rankin came in 1856 to this village from New York City, where he had been engaged in the crockery and glass ware trade. He quietly opened a small store in the Pumpelly Block and proceeded to build up a business. By honest dealing and close industry a living patronage was soon secured, and later years have brought further prosperity. In 1869, his son George S. Rankin, who had had an excellent business training of six years' duration with a large New York house in the same line, entered into the partnership, and through the joint efforts of father and son the volume of trade was much increased, the stock was enlarged and improved from time to time, and the commercial prosperity of the firm has continued to grow. Three years ago the block in which the store had all along been located was finely remodeled and improved. The front was rebuilt in the Queen Anne style, fine plate glass windows were made to replace the old-time windows with their small panes of common glass, and the exterior of the building became through these changes by far the handsomest in the village. A feature of the front worthy especial mention is that it possesses a large and fine sun dial, consisting of an extended bronze arm, in the hand of which is held an inverted lance, and beneath this is painted an arc upon which in gilt figures are the hours of the day, ranging from 1 to 12. The front is also decorated with fine colored glass from the works of the artist, John LaFarge. With the changes in the front of the block came other important improvements. The building was extended at the rear making its dimensions 100x33 feet, its floors and walls were renewed, and its appointments finely improved in all ways.

With the development of their trade the Rankins have come to occupy in addition to the fine main store of the block, the rear half of the adjoining store which is used as a packing room; the basement under both stores, where goods in bulk are stored, and a handsome display room on the second floor, 75x18 feet. A visit to this establishment reveals a most interesting and creditable display of the finest wares peculiar to the trade. Here are elegant Haviland china, in tea, fruit and dinner sets, beautiful Limoges and Faience goods rich Japanese porcelains, in salad bowls and after dinner coffees, fine hand painted Dresden china, in placques, vases, and salad bowls. Here also may be seen the newest designs in elegant library lamps of polished bronze, with prisms, vase lamps of real bronze in numerous striking designs, and other handsome vase lamps. A feature meriting special mention is a line of the finest polished cut glass-ware. These goods are the richest cutting produced, Tiffany, of New York, having nothing finer, and the cost is moderate when the quality of glass and the excellence of their cutting are taken into account. The long experience of the Messrs. Rankin in the trade has given them a wide acquaintance with leading dealers and manufacturers everywhere, and any articles not in their store can be procured by them promptly for their patrons, at the same price asked in the cities, and with the saving to buyers of freight and risk of transportation. In addition to a fine line of rich and costly goods, carried by Messrs. Rankin, they have in stock a great variety of English tea and dinner sets varying in cost from $5.00 to $65.00 a set, and a large assortment of the cheaper and more staple wares of the trade. A speciality is made of fine and useful wedding, holiday, and anniversary gifts. With such a stock to select from no one need find it necessary to go to the metropolis for fine presents. None of the near-by cities contain a store of the sort which carries as fine a line of rich goods. The establishment of Messrs. Rankin & Son is indeed a credit to Ithaca, and enterprise such as is displayed by this firm deserves the fullest support and encouragement.

JOHN NORTHRUP.

The business career of the subject of this sketch embraces a period of forty busy, prosperous years. John Northrup's first venture in a business way on his own account was made in 1843, when he bought the stock of Messrs. Hunter & Heggie contained in a store which formerly occupied the site of the present store of Samuel Harris, at 52 East State street. The stock consisted of trunks, harness, etc. and in connection with the sale of these goods, Mr. Northrup carried on the trade of carriage trimming. Two years and a half later he removed to the carriage shop of Wm. S. Hoyt, then occupying the ground where now stands Small's planing mill at the corner of Green and Tioga streets. In 1865 Mr. Northrup bought of the James S. Tichenor estate the brick block at the southeast corner of State and Aurora streets. There he began the sale of sewing machines, spring beds and Butterick's patterns, abandoning after a time the sale of harness, and work of carriage trimming. In 1876 he removed to a store in the Journal Block, which he occupied until May of this year, when he bought of J. M. Heggie, his fine store building, at 73 East State street, taking possession soon after. Thus after an interval of 40 years Mr. Northrup for a second time succeeded

Mr. Heggie, in the first instance to his stock in trade, and latterly to his store. He now deals extensively in the New Home and other sewing machines, spring beds, mattresses, and Butterick's fashion patterns.

E. W. PRAGER.

The business career of E. W. Prager covers a period of only eight years yet contains much that is of interest and has had in its progress not a few achievements upon which he may look with just pride. Mr. Prager was but seventeen years of age when he began to give instruction in dancing. In addition to his natural qualifications in the form of endurance and ease of motion, the young teacher displayed no small amount of patience and tact in imparting to pupils the principles of dancing. The result has been that he has had large success in this line of work. During the eight seasons which have passed since Mr. Prager's *debut* as a teacher of dancing he has given instruction to many hundreds of pupils in Ithaca, Cortland, Owego, Trumansburg, Farmer Village, and other surrounding places. He has made several trips to New York meanwhile to perfect himself in new styles of dancing and has continued to progress in his knowledge of the art, as well as his ability to instruct others in the acquirement of its rudiments, or carry them successfully through the more complicated steps and movements involved in the many prevailing styles of waltzes, and other difficult dances. While Mr. Prager has been making for himself an enviable standing in the art of dancing and its successful teaching, he has also been engaged in a number of business enterprises. For a time, in connection with J. H. Prager, he manufactured cigars, and during a year or two engaged in the traveling sale of these goods. In 1878, when the Lehigh Valley House was built, he became with his father joint proprietor of the business. Two years later he purchased the business and fine fittings of the Windsor restaurant, situated in the Clinton Block, on North Cayuga street. This is one of the most handsomely fitted and conveniently appointed restaurants in this locality. It is conducted in an excellent manner by Mr. Prager and enjoys a large and first-class patronage. As a member of the Ithaca Fire Department Mr. Prager has had considerable prominence for so young a man. Beginning as a lad in the capacity of torch boy to the chief, then Barnum R. Williams, he rose in a few years to be foreman of Torrent Hose Co. No. 5, and was elected to the office for three successive terms, viz, in 1878, 1879 and 1880. In 1881 he was chosen 2d assistant chief of the department, and in the following year he became 1st assistant chief. Although his name was prominently mentioned as a possible candidate for chief engineer at the expiration of his term as first assistant, his business and professional engagements were such as to make it unwise for him to accept the position, and he therefore declined to allow his name to be used. Something over a year ago Mr. Prager was tendered the position of drum major of the 50th Regiment Band, an excellent musical organization whose reputation is not by any means limited to this place. Although not familiar with the duties of the position when appointed, he began at once with customary energy to prepare himself for the creditable discharge of the requirements of the place. It was not long before he could wield the baton with the skill of a veteran. The uniform he purchased was one of the most showy and expensive owned by any drum major in the State. On parade, as in the ball room, Mr. Prager is graceful in movement, and in all respects makes a model drum major. Recently Mr. Prager was chosen business manager of the band, to succeed S. W. Walker. The readiness with which he adapts himself to new lines of work, and the large amount of energy which he possesses will make him a successful manager, and bring larger popularity and prosperity to the 50th Band.

NOURSE & DEDERER.

Several years ago a business was started by Charles M. Titus in the east store of the fine block on West State street bearing his name, which in the fall of 1881 passed into the hands of Messrs. Nourse & Dederer, and by them has been developed into a large and important enterprise. The business, as conducted by the present proprietors, consists of the manufacture of light and heavy platform wagons, fine buggies in many styles, and two-seated carriages. They are agents here for the celebrated Jackson lumber wagon, the Triumph reaper, Phelps chilled plow, Clipper mower, and Farmers' Friend grain drill. Their store, which is a very large one, contains a complete line of carriage goods of all kinds, horse clothing, harnesses, single and double, light and heavy, whips, brushes, etc. The establishment of Messrs. Nourse & Dederer is a first class one in all respects, and their stock not surpassed by that of any similar concern in this part of the state. It supplies a need long felt in this place, and the rapidly growing patronage of the firm is a forcible indication of the excellence of the goods handled, and of the thorough trustworthiness of the gentlemen who conduct the business.

JAMIESON & MC KINNEY.

It is a standing joke that plumbers invariably get very rich in a few years. While this is far from being true, there are occasionally cases, in which, as in other occupations, the honesty, fair-dealing, and enterprise of the plumber find just recognition at the hands of the public, and a fair amount of business prosperity is the result. The experience of the firm of Jamieson & McKinney, the well-known and reliable plumbers, gas and steam fitters, and wholesale dealers in plumber's goods, of this place, has fortunately been of this sort. In May, 1873, the senior member of this firm, John M. Jamieson, a practical plumber and gas fitter, bought of the Ithaca Gas & Water Company, their stock in trade and good will. There was at the time in the employ of the Gas & Water Company, a young man, who was recommended to Mr. Jamieson, as a faithful, valuable clerk and bookkeeper. The business prospered in Mr. Jamieson's hands from the first. From doing the bulk of the work in Ithaca, including the plumbing of a number of the many large and fine residences erected on East Hill during the last ten years, the business has extended into surrounding counties, in which many large contracts for steam and gas fitting have been skillfully and successfully executed. The plumbing of the splendid McGraw-Fiske mansion was done by Mr. Jamieson and his corps of workmen. In February, 1883, James A. McKinney, the young man who began with Mr. Jamieson, and had served faithfully and well during the preceding ten years, became a member of the firm. Jamieson & McKinney have now on hand the plumbing and steam fitting for the new Physical Laboratory of Cornell University, and the large depot building of the Lehigh Valley R. R. Co., at Wilkesbarre, Pa. They employ a force of from twelve to fifteen men, and are wholesale dealers in pipe, steam and gas fittings, and plumber's materials. All important work is done under the personal supervision of the senior member of the firm, who is one of the most experienced and successful workmen in his line in this section of the state. There is without doubt a long and highly successful business career in store for this pushing, worthy firm.

CENTRAL N. Y. ACCIDENT AND RELIEF ASSOCIATION.

The Central New York Accident and Relief Association of Ithaca opened their books for business in 1881. The founders are business men of Ithaca who felt confident that there was a demand for such an organization in Central New York. A charter was applied for and granted, permanently locating the organization in Ithaca. With but very little soliciting the society has grown to a membership of about 800, already giving a large insurance at a trifling cost. The amount of benefit will soon reach $2000 to the heirs of members in case of death, one-half of which is paid to the insured while living in case of permanent total disability by accident. The death assessment of the oldest member during the present year has been but $1.12 and to the youngest member but 50 cents. The schedule of assessments is equitably graded, ranging from 50 cents to $1.12 according to age. It comes within the ability of every laboring and business man to meet and thereby make extra provisions for his family against the day of adversity. Local boards have been established in nearly every town in this and adjoining counties. Newfield reports 60, Spencer 80, Waverly 54, Ithaca 120, other towns ranging from 10 to 25 members. The organization has every prospect of becoming one of the strongest as well as cheapest and most secure beneficiary societies in the state. The following are the directors and officers: Directors—**Levi Kenney**, Dr. E. J. Morgan, Sen., F. M. Bush, Dr. E. J. Morgan, Jr., O. P. Hyde, A. N. Hungerford, D. F. VanVleet, W. O. Wyckoff, George V. Benjamin, **George H. Northrup**, Ithaca ; **William F. Seeley**, Waverly. Officers—President, Levi Kenney ; Treasurer, George H. Northrup ; Medical Director, Dr. E. J. Morgan, Jr. ; General Agent, F. M. Bush ; Secretary and Superintendent of Agencies, George V. Benjamin.

HARRISON HOWARD.

The business of which **Harrison Howard is now** the sole proprietor has been in existence for sixty-one years, having been established by the late Frederick Deming in 1822. Originally the business was located in a store on the present site of the Deming Block, but later was removed to the storerooms now occupied. In 1857 Howard & Spencer purchased the business. Thomas Clement, of Lockport, N. Y., purchased Spencer's interest in 1861, and the firm of Howard & Clement conducted the business until September, 1882, since which time Mr. Howard has been the sole proprietor. This old established and favorably known house has for many years enjoyed an excellent patronage, and held its trade despite the efforts of pushing competitors. The line of goods in stock is very large and embraces, in addition to great quantities of staple wares, much rich and expensive furniture, and all that is desirable in the novelties of the trade. Mr. Howard has been not only a thorough and successful business man, but he has been one of the

strongest supporters of popular education. He was intimately associated with Mr. Cornell and other gentlemen in the formation of plans for the establishment of Cornell University and has always continued a staunch friend of the institution.

THE ITHACA HOTEL.

The great fire of August, 1871, destroying the old Ithaca Hotel, the large frame structure built in 1809 by Judge Gere, work was begun in the fall on the handsome five-story brick building now bearing the name and in 1872 it was completed at a cost of $64,000 and opened to the public, having been finely fitted up and furnished throughout. The old Ithaca Hotel had been popularly managed by Col. W. H. Welch since 1866, and a few years prior to its destruction Orlando B. Welch had been associated with his father in its management. Under the proprieship of Col. Welch & Son the new Ithaca was opened and successfully conducted until the death of Col. Welch in 1873, when a stock company bought the property and the proprietorship of the hotel passed into the hands of Alexander Sherman & Son, then recently proprietors of the Sherman House, Syracuse. In 1880 Frederick Sherman withdrew and returned to Syracuse, leaving the business here in the hands of his father, who has since had the entire charge of it. The large responsibilities and very considerable labor required in the management of this important enterprise, in which Mr. Sherman has for several years been assisted by Porter B. Jones, have of late weighed heavily on him, on account of his advancing years, and it is understood that he meditates retiring at no distant day from the conduct of this fine business. No house in this section of the State is more eligibly located, or better adapted to the enjoyment of a large and paying patronage, and with the growing business importance of Ithaca as well as the wider extension of the acquaintance of the public with the great natural attractions of this place and its vicinity as a summer resort, the business of the hotels in general, and of this fine property in particular is destined to greatly increase and prosper.

THOMAS F. DOHERTY.

From time to time there have been various billiard parlors in **operation in Ithaca**, some of which have had for a season a large patronage and have been the source of considerable profit to the proprietors. Possibly the most successful venture of this kind made here is the business conducted by **Thos. F.** Doherty in the Grant Block, over 14 and 16 East State street. **Mr. Doherty** began this business in the spring of **1879**, when four Collender billiard and two pool tables were put in to his parlors. The excellent manner in which the business was conducted, together with the superiority of the **tables and** equipments, and personal popularity of the proprietor soon won for his place a large and first class patronage, and this **prosperity has** continued steadily up to the present time. Recently the **rooms** were handsomely decorated and improved **making them** a model of attractive neatness.

THE TOMPKINS HOUSE.

This popular and well-known **hostlery** has a history running back to 1832, when a small one-story-and-a-half frame building **occupied** the site of the attractive four story structure now standing at the **northwest corner** of Seneca and Aurora streets. Very little change was made in the appearance of the premises until 1865, when Samuel Holmes and his son in-law, A. B. Stamp, **bought the property.** Messrs. Holmes & Stamp caused the house to be completely re-built, and greatly enlarged and improved the place. Under the direction of these well-**known and successful** proprietors the Tompkins House **soon became very popular, and a fine patronage was received.** Mr. Stamp's health failed after a few years and he was obliged **to** withdraw from **the** joint proprietorship of the house. After remaining several years on a farm, he returned to Ithaca and again became a part owner of the Tompkins House. In **1877** Mr Holmes withdrew, **leaving** Mr. Stamp to conduct the **business alone, and under** his capable management the Tompkins House has enjoyed for six years **an uninterrupted tide of** prosperity. Within the past year the house has undergone **a thorough renovation,** many improvements have been made, and **it is now one of the best hotels in** Ithaca.

E. K. JOHNSON.

One of the neatest and best kept retail groceries in Ithaca is the store of E. K. Johnson, located in the Hibbard Block at the corner of State and Cayuga streets. The site of the present store **is noted in the** history of Ithaca as the scene of **the** first murder occurring within the village precincts. In a small frame building which formerly stood on this ground, Guy C. Clark, a shoemaker, brutally killed his wife. Upon the completion of the brick block in 1847 the late **H. F. Hibbard** opened therein a general merchandise and variety store. **Upon** his sign was a bee hive and the busy, bustling appearance of the store at most times of the day or evening made this device significant and appropriate. The business passed successively through the hands **of** H. F. Hibbard, Hibbard & Atwater, Atwater & Nichols, Kenney, Byington & Co. and Col. K. S. Van Voorhees, who managed it as a co-operative store. In 1869 when this business was about to collapse the stock was purchased by the Johnson Brothers, E. K. and D. N. This copartnership continued until 1878, since which time the business has been conducted solely by E. K. Johnson, **who in addition** to being one of the most popular and thriving younger merchants of Ithaca, enjoys the distinction of having been one of the best County Treasurers Tompkins County ever had.

F. W. BROOKS.

No person with any natural refinement can enter a store such as that of F. W. Brooks, with its beautiful plate glass front, its glistening cases filled with rich silver ware, elegant jewelry, delicate china, and a host of attractive articles of kindred character, without experiencing a feeling of admiration and having his taste for the beautiful increased thereby. Its proprietor, Frederick W. Brooks, though still one of the younger business men of the place, has had a considerable practical experience. After a faithful apprenticeship of several years duration at the old established jewelry house of Joseph Burritt, Mr. Brooks in 1864 became a partner of J. C. Burritt, the firm name being Burritt, Brooks & Co. In 1875 he withdrew from this copartnership and taking the neat store at 50 East State street, began business on his own account. An excellent trade was established at this place but in course of time the business outgrew the dimensions of the store, and negotiations were opened with Judge D. Boardman for the lease of the store at 54 East State street, which was then in course of repair and improvement. This attractive place of business Mr. Brooks took possession of in November, 1882. Many of his friends predicted that disaster would follow this movement, but his enterprise, however, did not bring him loss. On the contrary, a much larger patronage was soon secured. A glance through the establishment now reveals a most attractive display of rich wares. Here are watches in great variety, fine jewelry, diamonds, silver and plated ware, fine table cutlery, beautiful lamps of unique design and richest workmanship, delicate Sevres, and Limoges China and Wedgwood ware, porcelain placques, and a host of other elegant and expensive articles. In the department of engraving and repairing the most skillful workmanship is displayed. Mr. Brooks retaining the services in this connection of his brother, C. H. Brooks, an experienced practical jeweler. No finer selection of wedding, birthday or holiday presents could be made in the metropolis than may be had at this finely conducted store. It is a pleasure to write of a business so admirably complete in all its features as that which has been briefly described in this sketch and a high degree of success is justly due its worthy proprietor.

PARIS & EMIG.

The shaving and bathing establishment of Messrs. Paris & Emig located in the Ithaca Hotel Block is probably the largest and most completely appointed shop of the kind in any of the smaller cities of the State. The copartnership existing between Harry Paris and Adam Emig was formed in 1878. The fine rooms in the Hotel Block were completely refitted and finely improved making them the handsomest place for the business of any in this section of the State. By close attention to business and the most capable management a large patronage was soon secured and the excellent reputation early obtained has been continuously enjoyed and a large and growing trade is now done at this establishment. Six expert barbers are employed, the bath rooms are finely conducted and in all respects the shop of Paris & Emig is a first-class one and worthy of continued prosperity.

W. H. WILLSON.

Among the many first-class mercantile establishments in Ithaca, none are more deserving of mention in this work than the store of W. H. Willson, in the Sprague Block, No. 51 East State street. This is one of the most elegant stores in the village and contains a stock of hats, caps, gloves, furs and robes that would only be expected from such an establishment in the larger cities. It is undoubtedly the largest stock of these goods in the county, and the fact that many country merchants come here to lay in their stock is an evidence that the stock and prices are appreciated. Mr. Willson's trade is both wholesale and retail. He is a native of Ithaca, and for a number of years was a commercial traveler for a prominent New York house. In 1868 he returned to his native place and opened a hat store in a building near the old Ithaca Hotel. Three years ago he secured the elegant storeroom in the Sprague Block and here his business has largely increased, as it properly should with such splendid facilities for making a pleasing display of goods, and he is now recognized as the leader in this particular line of trade in this section.

J. T. MORRISON.

One of the most successful merchants in Ithaca, J. T Morrison can look back with pride upon the many years he has spent in the mercantile trade. When quite a young boy he began his apprenticeship as a clerk in the service of Ludlowville and Rochester merchants. Four years of his early life was thus passed in gaining a knowledge of busines affairs, and after three more years thus given to the acquirement of experience—the latter three at the store of Finch & Stowell, where the store of Marsh & Hall now stands—he embarked in business for himself at Ludlowville, in 1851. For seven years he conducted business there with much success, and in 1858 removed to Ithaca and formed the co-partnership of Morrison, Woodworth & Granger, at No. 22 East State street. In 1860 the firm was changed to Morrison & Woodworth, and in 1861 it became Morrison, Hawkins & Co. At this location Mr. Morrison continued until 1869, when he resolved to be his own partner, and severing his connections with the firm of Morrison, Hawkins & Co., opened a store at the corner of Tioga and State streets, his present location. Just at this time the great shrinkage in the value of merchandise occurred which proved disastrous to so many merchants throughout the country, and it was then he displayed his peculiar adaptability for business, for despite the unfavorable condition of affairs in the country, he successfully passed through the ordeal and probably made more money than at any time during his previous business experience. Again in 1873, was he severely tried, a portion of his store building being burned to the ground, entailing considerable loss, but he was equal to the occasion, and immediately re-building began business with renewed vigor. Success has since uniformly marked his career, and to-day he occupies a position that is unassailable. Originally dealing in dry goods exclusively, about eight years ago Mr. Morrison added carpets to his stock, and last year in pursuance of the policy of his competitors, added merchant tailoring, employing his own cutter and making the department complete. Two storerooms, forming an *L*, are occupied, the entrance to the dry goods department being on State, and to the merchant tailoring department on Tioga street. The basement is occupied by the carpet department. Large and fine stocks of goods fill every department, and it is safe to say there is not an establishment in the village in which the details are more closely looked after or that is better managed. The business this year is showing an increase of nearly 50 per cent over preceding ones, and the sales will probably amount to $65,000 for the year.

JAMES QUIGG.

David Quigg was a native of New Hampshire, and one of those sturdy young men who form the pioneer element in new and unimproved countries. He was born in 1781 and was only eighteen years of age when he left his home to become one of the settlers in the then uninhabited wilds of Central New York. He bought a piece of land near Spencer and had cleared off a portion of it when he became somewhat dissatisfied with his land on account of its stony nature and returned to his "down East" home. He was much attracted, however, by the opportunities offered in this new country and in 1801 returned. Mr. Quigg bought a piece of land on the south side of Cascadilla Creek, just opposite Williams' Cascadilla Mills, and building upon it a log structure he opened the first store in which goods were offered for sale in this vicinity. Every merchantable article was kept on sale—to eat, to drink, to heal the sick, clothe the body or till the soil. Here he remained in business for some years and when the village began to grow he moved to Seneca street, opposite the present site of the Tompkins House. He retired from business with a competence in 1848 and left his store in the hands of his sons, J. W. and James Quigg. In 1853 they removed to No. 32 East State street, where the business was continued by the brothers as a firm until 1865, since which time it has been conducted by James Quigg alone. David Quigg died in 1862, having lived to see the village in which he opened the first store when it contained only two or three houses, become one of the largest and most prosperous villages in New York, and his son occupying the same position, relatively, to its business interests that he did when he was a young man and the village was in its infancy. The business of James Quigg is in a flourishing condition, and the recollections of himself and his deceased father, could they be obtained, would form a complete history of the "Forest City," for in father and son has been witnessed its rise, progress and growth.

H. M. STRAUSSMAN.

The "Banner Clothing Store" is so well known to all residents of Tompkins County that a brief sketch of the establishment and its proprietor will prove of interest to many readers. Mr. H. M. Straussman is a native of Germany, and came to Ithaca from New York City about twelve years ago. Pleased with the locality, he opened a store on State street for the sale of ready-made clothing and merchant tailoring. The goods in which he dealt, and the principles upon which his business was conducted, merited and met with popular approval, and as a consequence new customers were constantly being added to his list of patrons. His business steadily increased and his success as a clothier became so marked as to draw to his store the best class of custom. About four years ago, his business having entirely outgrown the quarters occupied, he secured the three story building at No. 40 East State street and fitted it up for conducting the business on a large scale. Here his success has been still more marked, and it has come to be acknowledged that he has secured the position of the leading clothier in Ithaca by his enterprise and appreciation of the wants of the people. The building in which is the "Banner Clothing Store" is a fine three-story brick structure and gives excellent opportunities for the manufacture and display of goods. The first floor is devoted to the display of ready made suitings and gents' furnishing goods. On the second floor are shown overcoats and cloths. The third floor is occupied by the tailoring department. Mr. Straussman employs eighteen people and is undoubtedly the largest and leading clothier in the county. It is well known that he has always kept the better grades of ready made clothing, and in the merchant tailoring department principally imported goods are made up. To the knowledge of these facts by the people he is doubtless largely indebted for his success. That this success will continue and he retain the position he has gained and now occupies, as the leader in this trade, there is no doubt in the minds of those who are acquainted with Mr. Straussman and his honorable methods of doing business.

CONCLUSION.

My task is done. If you have continued with me from the beginning, remained my companion through all my ramble in and about the "Forest City," you must now be of the opinion that Ithaca is more than an "obscure village in the central part of New York;" that it is really an industrial, as well as an educational centre of importance, and that here is one of the most striking combinations of romantic scenery, advanced industry and educational development to be found in all this great country. And now I will say adieu, hoping that I have not only interested you, but that my work will prove beneficial to the village of Ithaca as well as to you, by thus calling your attention to the "Forest City" and its numerous attractions.

www.ingramcontent.com/pod-product-compliance
Lightning Source LLC
Chambersburg PA
CBHW021941160426
43195CB00011B/1177